GUARANTEED TO LAST

L.L.BEAN's CENTURY *of* OUTFITTING AMERICA

by JIM GORMAN

L.L.Bean   MELCHER MEDIA

L.L.Bean
Creative Director: Jenna Klein Jonsson
Project Support: Kathleen Dougherty

Produced by  MELCHER MEDIA

124 West 13th Street
New York, NY 10011
www.melcher.com

Publisher: Charles Melcher
Associate Publisher: Bonnie Eldon
Editor in Chief: Duncan Bock
Senior Editor: David Brown
Project Editor: Lauren Nathan
Editorial Intern: Austin O'Malley

Production Director: Kurt Andrews
Production Associate: Daniel Del Valle

Interior Design by Think Studio, NYC
Creative Director: John Clifford

Cover Design by Paul Kepple of Headcase Design

Distributed by Perseus Distribution

10 9 8 7 6 5 4 3 2 1

Printed in China

ISBN: 978-1-59591-070-7

Library of Congress Control Number: 2011941248

CONTENTS

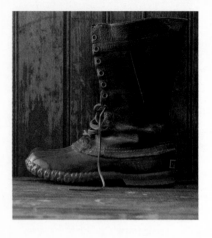

FOREWORD

A LOT HAS BEEN WRITTEN OVER THE YEARS ABOUT MY GRANDFATHER, L.L. BEAN, THE MAN, AS WELL AS THE COMPANY HE STARTED. I'VE WRITTEN MY SHARE ABOUT BOTH FOR VARIOUS SPEECHES AND PUBLICATIONS, INCLUDING *L.L.BEAN: THE MAKING OF AN AMERICAN ICON* (PUBLISHED IN 2006). THE STORY OF L.L.BEAN IS AN EVER-EVOLVING ONE, WITH LESSONS TO BE LEARNED FOR ALL GENERATIONS IN VERY APPEALING AND HUMAN TERMS. THIS LATEST VERSION IS ONE OF THE BEST.

Guaranteed to Last, by Jim Gorman (no relation), is introduced here with much appreciation for a job well done and with great enthusiasm for its fresh insights into L.L. and his values-based company. This is all very fitting, since Jim's rendition of the company's story commemorates our one-hundredth anniversary. Jim tells the story in the context of America's varied outdoor interests and passions over the past century. He weaves the themes that link L.L.Bean with its loyal customers and their lifestyles. They, and our committed employees, play an active part in Jim's narrative through interviews and anecdotes. They continue to live the values and share the bedrock beliefs of L.L.Bean as it evolves into the twenty-first century.

The values are derived from the L.L. story: of pithy advice, like "If you get lost in the woods, come straight back to camp"; of the outdoors and the first leather-top, rubber-bottom boot discovery; of the first one hundred pairs and the birth of the 100 percent guarantee; of the best service and a deep and abiding respect for people—and of L.L.'s revolutionary idea of caring enough to treat a customer like a human being.

People often ask me what, if L.L. were alive today, he would think of his company and what we've done with it. I think he'd be a little taken aback at the technology, but on the whole would say the values are intact, we've been true to his legacy, and he'd be pleased that the Maine Hunting Shoe is still made in the good old state of Maine, U.S.A.

As we aspire to another century of L.L.Bean, we hope to proudly say the same the next time around.

–*Leon Gorman, Chairman of the Board, L.L.Bean*

CHAPTER 1

BIRTH OF THE BOOT

The **MAINE HUNTING SHOE** | First sold in **1912**

AN OUTDOORSMAN FIRST AND BUSINESSMAN SECOND, L.L. BEAN HAD RETURNED FROM TOO MANY HUNTING TRIPS WITH COLD, WET, CHAFED FEET. HE WANTED A COMFORTABLE BOOT THAT WOULD STAND UP TO THE ELEMENTS. AS HE WOULD FIND OUT, HE WASN'T ALONE. WITHIN A DECADE OF BUILDING THE FIRST MAINE HUNTING SHOE, BEAN HAD A THRIVING MAIL-ORDER OPERATION CATERING TO THOSE WHO SHARED HIS LOVE OF NATURE—AND THE BEGINNINGS OF WHAT WOULD BECOME AN INTERNATIONAL OUTFITTER.

All Leon Leonwood Bean wanted was a better boot. One that would keep his feet dry in the woods and marshes of Maine. He didn't imagine his innovative footwear would sell by the millions or still be crafted in essentially identical form a hundred years later. He surely couldn't have known the company bearing his name would grow into one of America's most recognized and admired brands. Or that his way of doing business would make him a legend in his own time, leading the *Wall Street Journal* to enshrine him atop its list of the century's most

Above: In 1902, L.L. operates a horse-drawn wagon for the early Bean Brothers' pant store located in Auburn, Maine. Below: A Bean Brothers' baseball bat. Opposite: L.L. models his first Maine Safety Hunting Coat in 1917.

transformational entrepreneurs — ahead of Bill Gates and Sam Walton.

Like self-made men before him and after, L.L., as he insisted everyone call him, benefited from a measure of luck and good timing. And without doubt, his perseverance, self-confidence, and daring contributed to his success. Such up-by-the-bootstraps, small-town-boy-makes-good stories are the stuff of American folklore. The real genius of L.L., what sets him apart, is the extent to which he put bedrock values like trust and respect at the heart of his enterprise. Doing

things the right way was the only way for L.L., and he proved it was good business practice, too. A century later, those same values still guide his company.

At the moment the bolt of inspiration struck L.L., very little in his background suggested he might someday lead a multimillion-dollar company. In fact, L.L.'s history should hearten late bloomers everywhere. The year was 1911 and he was by then a middle-aged man of forty. Stints working at shoe and apparel shops around Maine for his brother Otho and W.H. Moody, prior to running his own shoe and men's furnishing store in Freeport, gave L.L. plenty of retail experience and paid the bills. But his work wasn't nearly as satisfying as his true passion for pursuing big game and trout in remotest Maine. L.L. lived for weekends and long vacations filled with the thrill of the chase and easy camaraderie among fellow hunters. He was just back from such a hunting expedition up north—footsore once again from wearing clunky leather boots that leaked and then stiffened painfully as they dried—when he got a bright idea.

"I was quite interested in getting the right kind of footwear for deer hunting," he would write decades later in his autobiography, *My Story: The Autobiography of a Down-East Merchant*. "I took a pair of shoe rubbers from the stock on the shelves and had a shoe maker cut out a pair of 7½" tops. The local cobbler stitched the whole thing together." New England's notoriously rugged, boggy terrain was about to meet its match.

L.L. didn't intend his comfortable, waterproof creation for anyone's use but his own, and it might have languished if local dairyman Edgar Conant hadn't stepped through the door at L.L. Bean Clothier on Freeport's Main Street that

Off and on from 1897 to 1907, L.L. recorded entries in a hunting diary. In addition to records of his kills, he included photos and weather information.

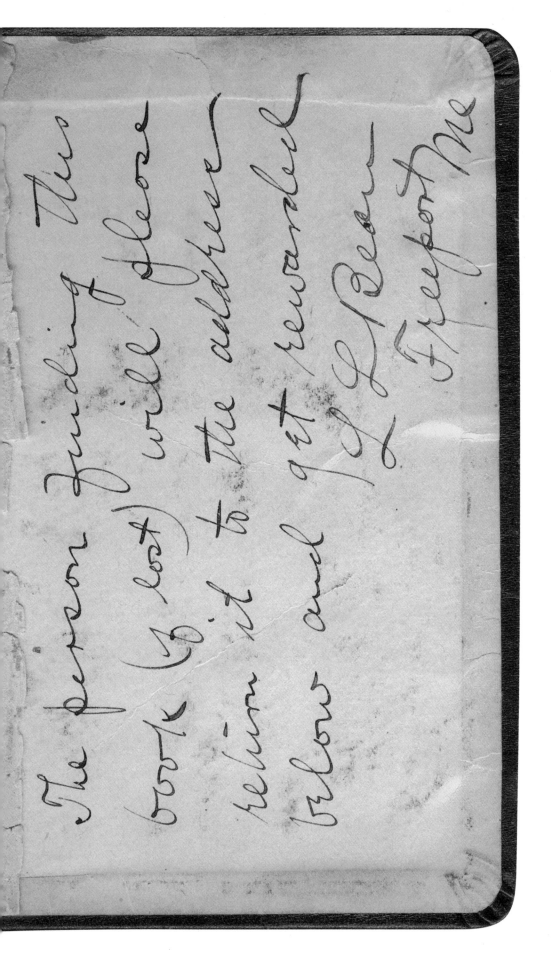

The person finding this book (if lost) will please return it to the address below and get rewarded

L L Bean Freeport Me

AT 13,
L.L. SHOT
HIS FIRST
DEER ON
A HUNT-
ING TRIP
WITH HIS
COUSIN,
AND A
LIFELONG
PASSION
WAS BORN.

Above: In the fall of 1911, prototypes of the Maine Hunting Shoe got an early "field test." From left to right are L.L. Bean, Benjamin Swett (L.L.'s uncle), Levi Patterson, and Louvie Swett (L.L.'s cousin). Opposite: An early ad for the Maine Hunting Shoe.

September. As the two got to talking, "I quite innocently praised my new shoe," recalled L.L. Conant asked to try a pair, and L.L. happily obliged. Months later a package arrived at L.L.'s store. Inside were the boots and a note from Conant: "I wore these shoes two weeks moose hunting last October and then put them right into hard service on the milk farm right up to the first of March. Your shoe is not only O.K. for hunting, but is the lightest and best wearing farm shoe I ever had." Conant wasn't giving back the boots. He wanted their worn rubber bottoms replaced and returned as soon as possible.

"From his recommendation," said L.L. in classic understatement, "I decided I had struck the right thing in the great hunting ground of the state of Maine."

Something in Conant's feedback clearly resonated within L.L. His entrepreneurial drive was sprung loose, and the course of L.L.'s life veered onto a new path. Perhaps it was the validation L.L. felt for his very personal creation, or maybe it was something deeper in a grown man who had been orphaned at age twelve and was then compelled to spend his youth obligingly working on neighbors' and relatives' farms. L.L., never one to talk about himself, was mum on the subject. Drew Hansen, who blogs about entrepreneurship for *Forbes,* offers insight. Entrepreneurs, he says, are engaged in a form of self-expression not unlike an artist's. Their work is an extension of themselves and "springs from their deepest yearnings, making it unique and personal. There is no guarantee that the

With Heels 25c. Extra

MAINE
HUNTING SHOE

—

WEIGHS ONLY 33 OUNCES TO THE PAIR.

OUTSIDE of your gun, nothing is so important to your outfit as your foot-wear. You cannot expect success hunting big game if your feet are not properly dressed.

The Maine Hunting Shoe is designed by a hunter who has tramped Maine woods for the past nineteen years. They are as light as a pair of moccasins with the protection of a heavy hunting boot.

My new improved 1914 shoes are made on a swing last that fits the foot like a dress shoe and comes in three heights, 8, 11 and 14 inch, also three widths, medium, narrow and wide. The tops are soft Water Elk that never grow hard by wetting and drying. The vamps are the very best gum rubber money will buy. The soles are white rolled edge gum rubber. Leather innersoles keep the feet off the rubber and prevent "drawing" that is so objectionable with most rubber shoes.

For those hunters who go just before the first snow it is next to impossible to find footwear that is adapted to both bare ground and snow hunting. The Maine Hunting Shoe is perfect for both. For bare ground, its extreme light weight and leather inner soles keep it from drawing the feet while the rubber soles keep it from slipping. For snow, by using a heavier stocking you have warm, light dry footwear that is ideal for still hunting.

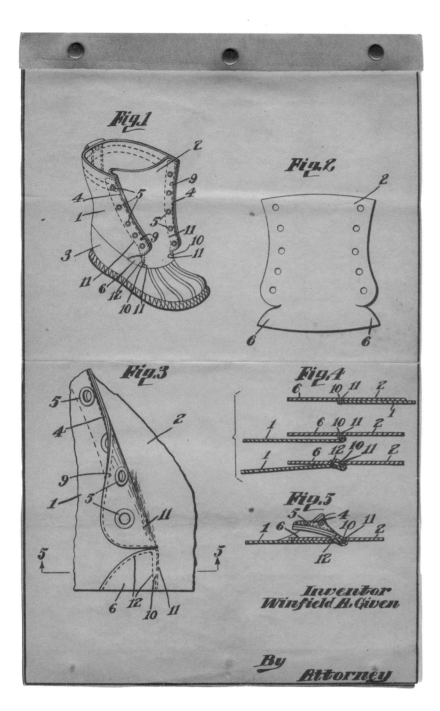

UNITED STATES PATENT OFFICE.

LEON L. BEAN, OF FREEPORT, MAINE.

SPLIT BACKSTAY.

1,365,080. Specification of Letters Patent. Patented Jan. 11, 1921.

Application filed June 11, 1920. Serial No. 388,293.

To all whom it may concern:

Be it known that I, LEON L. BEAN, a citizen of the United States, residing at Freeport, in the county of Cumberland and State 5 of Maine, have invented certain new and useful Improvements in Split Backstays, of which the following is a specification.

The present invention relates to boot and shoe constructions, and has more particular 10 reference to an improved back stay and top construction.

An object of the present invention is to provide a construction of back stay which will prevent what is known as heel cord 15 chafing, usually produced by the set wrinkles which form directly over the heel cords and which break and chafe the stitches, and not only make the shoe uncomfortable but also weak at this particular point.

20 Another object of the invention is to provide a shoe construction wherein the shoe is relatively strong and protected at the point of application of the back stay; wherein the improved construction admits of use 25 of waste or small pieces of stock; wherein the top may be stitched onto the shoe or vamp quicker and in a more satisfactory manner; and wherein there is avoided the bringing together of double thicknesses of 30 leather or rubber at the same point as is required with the present day shoe construction; and wherein a single thickness of leather is provided at the back of the shoe and the usual thick lip is done away with 35 which catches in hard snow or crust and gradually tears the top away from the lower part of the shoe.

The above, and various other objects and advantages of this invention will be in part 40 described in, and in part understood from, the following detail description of the present preferred embodiment, the same being illustrated in the accompanying drawing, wherein—

45 Figure 1 is a perspective view of a shoe constructed according to the present invention, the view being from the back of the shoe.

Fig. 2 is a detail enlarged fragmentary 50 view of the top part of the shoe at the heel thereof, shown in a partly stitched condition.

Fig. 3 is a transverse section through the heel part of the shoe taken through the back 55 stay.

Referring to the drawing, there is shown, for the purpose of setting forth the present invention, a shoe of the type which is known as a hunting shoe, and wherein the sole 10 and vamp 11 are made substantially integral 60 and of rubber, and wherein the top portion of the shoe is made of leather.

In the present instance the top is made from the side pieces 12 and 13 of leather or the like and which are stitched together at 65 the back of the shoe against the inner side of a back stay 14. According to the present invention the back stay 14 is split or divided at its lower end into downwardly diverging branches 15 having an angle of divergence 70 sufficient to carry the lower ends of the branches 15 toward the sides of the heel part so as to leave a relatively broad V-shaped space within the lower end of the back stay 14. 75

As best shown in Fig. 3, the side pieces 12 and 13 of the top are cut away at their meeting edges on the lines of divergence of the back stay 14 and a third piece 16 of leather or the like is inserted in the opening or space 80 between the lower end portions of the parts 12 and 13 to act as a filler and a continuation of the parts which combine to make the top of the shoe. The part 16 constitutes the back of the heel top and is preferably of the 85 same material as the sides 12 and 13 and is flexible and capable of bending and conforming to the heel of the wearer and to the creases imposed upon the heel part incident to the use of the shoe. The lateral edge por- 90 tions of the part 16 are stitched along the inner marginal edge portions of the branches 15 of the back stay and abut against the adjacent edges of the side pieces 12 and 13 and are preferably secured thereto by lines of 95 stitching 17.

The top of the shoe is secured by lines of stitching 18 to the upper edge of the shoe vamp 11. In the present instance the shoe vamp is of rubber and consequently the lines 100 of stitching 18 may, in ordinary shoe construction, be easily broken away at the heel of the shoe.

As may be best understood from Fig. 3, the vamp 11 of the shoe provides a thick- 105 ness at the heel and the rear part 16 of the top merely adds an additional thickness to the heel of the shoe so that there is the least possible multiplicity of layers of material at the heel of the shoe where the wrinkles 110

audience or market will accept their work," writes Hansen. And so an entrepreneur's true self is exposed and at risk of rejection.

Resolved, L.L. put together a plan to market his boot, which he had taken to calling the Maine Hunting Shoe. Not content to sell a few pairs of the boot from his shop to local farmers and woodsmen, L.L. dreamed bigger. And mail order, a relatively new way of conducting business popularized by catalogers Montgomery Ward and Sears, Roebuck, and Company on a nationwide scale, would be his tool. The open question was how to find the names and addresses of potential customers in an era before rentable, computerized mailing lists? L.L. hit on the idea of drawing from Maine's list of nonresident hunters, who he knew had to apply for a special license. Anyone who traveled to Maine to hunt had to be a passionate outdoorsman of some means.

"The Maine Hunting Shoe is designed by a hunter who has tramped Maine woods for the past eighteen years," read the promotional letter L.L. crafted and mailed off to one thousand out-of-staters. Just a single sheet of paper folded in half, the circular had room for a testimonial from Edgar Conant, a typewritten and signed note from L.L., and promotional copy pitching the

boot. Already L.L.'s flair for direct, personalized salesmanship, which would become a hallmark of the L.L.Bean catalog, was evident: "For all-round hunting purposes there is not a shoe on the market at any price equal to the Maine Hunting Shoe."

Another obstacle L.L. had to hurdle was the sullied reputation of circularizing, or selling through the mail. It's called "direct marketing" today. According to Ray Schultz, president of TellAll marketing and former editor of *Direct Marketing News*, scams involving lotteries and potion cures for cancer, dyspepsia, and drunkenness, as well as get-rich-quick schemes, were rife at the turn of the last century. Some of the worst abuses emanated from Augusta, Maine. "The pioneers of direct marketing were a bunch of crooks," says Schultz. The U.S. Post Office and the Pure Food and Drug Act of 1906 cracked down on the most egregious offenders, but the buying public was leery, particularly of any unsolicited letter postmarked from Maine.

L.L. needed a way to assure perfect strangers that they could buy from him in confidence. He decided to vouch for his boots with a guarantee printed on a tag, which read: "We guarantee this pair of shoes to give perfect satisfaction in every

Opposite, top: Improvements to the tongue of the Maine Hunting Shoe are documented in a 1921 patent and its accompanying sketch. Opposite, bottom: A patent for the Shoe's "Split Backstay," which prevented heel chafing, also from 1921. Above: Early views of the L.L.Bean store (at left, L.L. is standing in the doorway).

THE MacMILLAN ARCTIC ASSOCIATION

626 TREMONT BUILDING, BOSTON, MASS.

Mr. L. L. Bean,
Freeport,
Maine.

June 20, 1923

Dear Sir:

Enclosed find order for 7 pair Maine Hunting Shoes with Non-Slip sole for myself and crew.

My men are very enthusiastic over their experience with your foot equipment on our last Arctic Expedition, finding it extremely practical, especially for fall and spring work.

I believe that the new crepe sole Hunting Shoe which we are ordering this year will be even more popular with my men, if such can be possible.

The rocky frozen ground of Ellesmere Land, where we are planning to winter within twelve degrees of the Pole, is the very hardest kind of a test on the wearing qualities of foot gear. You may look for an interesting report upon my return home in the fall of 1924.

Very truly yours,

DBM:L

D. B. MacMillan

1923

100 YEARS OF DRY FEET

WHEN YOU'VE BEEN AROUND AS LONG AS THE BEAN BOOT,
PEOPLE START TALKING.

"Enclosed please find one 35 mm slide of a distinguished group of Missouri fishermen who posed for this shot at Big Canon Lake in Ontario last summer.

This group has been fishing together for several years. At first just one or two of us had Bean Hunting Boots. Little by little the great Bean tradition spread so that by this year all of us were sporting the same unbeatable quality that typifies the Bean Hunting Boot."

—Richard B., M.D., Liberty, Missouri,
March 4, 1984

"I have enclosed a photo of a framed picture of my grandfather, Frederic Ewing, taken at his hunting lodge in Maine in the 1950s. I found the picture in the basement of my mother's home in Boothbay Harbor after she passed away. When I recognized the boots he's wearing as L.L.Bean boots, I had to share it with you. As you can see, our family has been loyal customers for quite awhile."

—Polly A., Virgina Beach, Virginia
January 17, 2009

"The year was 1979; I was crazy about this girl I had just met in high school. One Saturday after taking our SAT exams, I asked her if she wanted a ride home. When she accepted my offer, I asked her if she wanted to join me in a ride to L.L.Bean first so that I could get a new pair of Bean Boots.

To my good fortune and thirty-two years later, I still have that same pair of boots. And that same great girl! (OK, the boots have been resoled once or twice.) My wife and I still enjoy our many visits to Bean and appreciate the quality in all things we've gotten there over the years. Many thanks."

—"JL1979" (from website),
Freeport, Maine, April 3, 2011

way. If the rubber breaks or the tops grow hard, return them, together with this guarantee tag, and we will replace them free of charge."

Orders streamed in, one hundred in all. "I hired Ted Goldrup to cut, and his wife to stitch the tops. With the local cobbler attaching the tops to the rubbers, I was in the mail-order business," said L.L. His novel solution to an age-old problem of cold, wet feet would in time alter his personal fortunes and others', and help establish one of the longest-lived and best-loved companies in America.

It would have been a great, simple story about invention and success. But there was one hitch: the first version of the Maine Hunting Shoe was a bust. Of the one hundred pairs of boots L.L. sold at $3.50 apiece, ninety blew apart. Their owners returned the damaged goods to Freeport for a refund. "The idea was all right but the rubber was not strong enough to hold the

'stitched on' tops," admitted L.L. in retrospect. The Maine Hunting Shoe was guaranteed "to give satisfaction in every way." It nearly put him out of business.

Bruised but nonetheless optimistic, L.L. wasn't about to give up. Successful entrepreneurs are that way. "Failure," said Henry Ford, "is simply the opportunity to begin again, this time more intelligently." And L.L. did. He saw great market potential for his unique boot if he could find a sturdier yet still lightweight rubber bottom. With $400 borrowed from his brother Otho, L.L. journeyed to Boston to strike a deal with the giant U.S. Rubber Company. "The kind of last [foot form] I wanted was so expensive the company wanted a much larger order than I could afford. I went home and raised more money, and not too easily convinced them that my shoe would be a winner."

The small workshop in the basement of L.L.'s

Opposite: *The Moose Hunter*, 1921, William Harnden Foster (1886–1941), oil on canvas. The image graced the cover of a 1925 catalog. Above right: A 1917 L.L.Bean jacket donated to the company archives by Holly Stover of Richmond, Massachusetts. Above left: Stover's grandfather, Frank Howard, the coat's original owner.

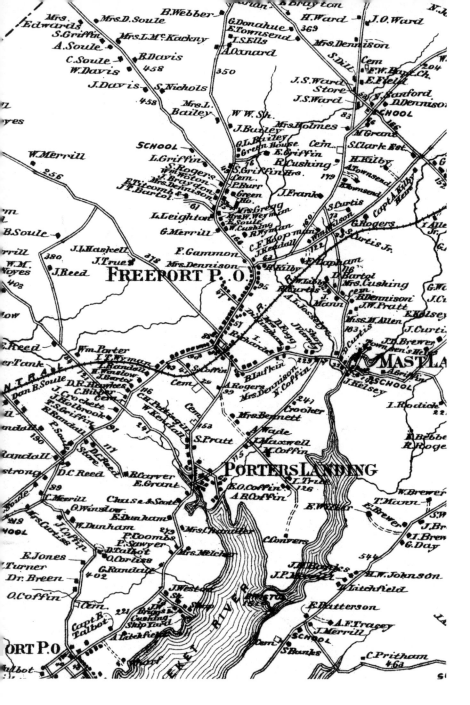

store, where the Maine Hunting Shoe was assembled and boxed for shipment, soon buzzed with activity. "I secured heavier rubbers, improved the tops, invented and patented numerous items that made the Maine Hunting Shoe unexcelled," recounted L.L. A trickle of new orders stimulated by advertisements placed in *National Sportsman*, *Field & Stream*, and other publications soon became a torrent.

By summer 1917, L.L.'s sideline operation at his haberdashery was bursting out of the basement. To make room for more boot makers and additional storage, L.L. leased the top floor of the building across Main Street, to this day the current site of the L.L.Bean retail store. "By the next January business had grown to such proportions that I sold the retail store in order to devote my whole time to the mail-order business I had built up," said L.L. The orders kept streaming in. By early 1920, the Maine Hunting Shoe was joined by the Maine Hunting Pant, Maine Auto Sweater, and fifteen other items in L.L.'s catalog of outdoors essentials.

Squeezed again by piled-up boxes of inventory and an expanded workforce, L.L. made the leap from renter to owner by purchasing the entire Warren Block building for $7,883.64. The top two floors would house L.L.Bean; the ground floor was rented to the Freeport post office. As the volume of outgoing packages grew, the addition of a chute to the post office below saved everyone time and prevented the occasional dropped box when shipping clerks teetered down the stairs carrying overloaded wicker baskets full of parcels.

Recounting those early days with the benefit of hindsight in his autobiography *My Story*, published in 1960, L.L. was rightly proud if not a bit dazzled by his success. "There are few enterprises that begin so modestly and grow so rapidly," he wrote.

....

Above: Map of Freeport, 1871.
Opposite: Early images of Freeport, including, at bottom, the rebuilt Davis Block and Clark's Hotel in 1912.

Not merely content to sell a few p
to local farmers and

...irs of the boot from his shop
...woodsmen, L.L. dreamed bigger.

L. L. BEAN INC. FREEPORT MAINE

A lot can change in a century. Go back in time one hundred years to find Woodrow Wilson, then governor of New Jersey, campaigning for the White House. Everyone aspired to own a Model T or Hudson 20 Roadster. New York and Cleveland had banned a scandalous new dance from Argentina, the tango. Gentlemen wore top hats and frock coats; ladies flaunted exotic feathered hats. Charlie Chaplin, not yet a silent-movie star, was playing music halls. And the unsinkable *Titanic* was about to embark from Southampton, England, to New York.

What little remains from that distant era can often only really be found in museums. In a bustling factory on the outskirts of Brunswick, Maine, however, the past is very much alive. Inside, forty-five workers go through twenty-eight steps necessary to sew together the Maine Hunting Shoe and its close relation, the Bean Boot. There's more automation and people power involved, but it's a hands-on process L.L. would recognize. Through two world wars, the Great Depression, the Cold War, the upheaval of the 1960s, plus untold changes in fashion, the Maine Hunting Shoe has remained in continuous production. Far from fading into obscurity, the Maine Hunting Shoe–Bean Boot is riding a surge in popularity, selling more pairs in 2010 than ever before.

What explains such longevity? It starts with delivering an honest product at an honest price. The Maine Hunting Shoe is foremost about performance: lightweight, water-resistant, form-fitting, grippy, and long-wearing. L.L. designed his boot to give hunters the element of surprise while moving through a forest courtesy of a soft, flexible moccasin-like sole that allows the wearer to sense any stick that might snap or rock that

Winter Sport Cap

Is made of high grade Mahogany glove leather, trimmed with the very best white lamb-skin, that looks and feels like fur.

Visor can be worn up or down.

A very practical, sporty looking cap for Snow-shoeing, Skiing, Skating and other winter sports. With ear protectors down it looks like a high grade aviator's cap and will keep head, neck and ears warm in the very coldest weather.

Outside of our Hunting Shoe, Leather Caps are the biggest sellers we manufacture.

Weight only 6 oz. Price, $3.85, delivered. Send for free samples of leather and lamb-skin.

We also make to order Olive Green and Dark Red Caps trimmed with White Lambskin, as shown on back cover.

Showing Cap with ear protectors and visor up

$3.85 Postpaid

Showing Cap with ear protectors down

Bean's New Deer Hunting Cap $2.50 Postpaid

As shown at left, gives almost absolute protection against accidental shooting.

Made of fine all wool red felt with black Elk leather band and visor.

Do not take chances hunting big game without red Cap or Coat.

Cap at right is made of best mahogany Elk leather with red leather band and wool ear laps.

Gives better protection than a cloth cap, will not catch or brush off in thick bushes; is water-proof and will last a lifetime.

We want you to see these caps. Order one and return it after your trip, if you are not more than satisfied. Weight, 5 ounces. Send for free sample of leather and felt. Made-to-order in Black with Red band.

$2.50 Postpaid

Showing ear laps down

Manufactured and sold by   L. L. BEAN, FREEPORT, MAINE

Left: A Bean's Winter Sports Cap (top) and New Deer Hunting Cap (bottom) from the 1920s. Above: Versions of both caps in the 1926 L.L.Bean catalog. Opposite: An early catalog guarantee; the sole of a pre-1935 Maine Hunting Shoe. (The company added "Inc." after L.L.Bean in 1934.)

MAKING WEARABLE HISTORY

Building the Bean Boot today involves more automation, higher volume (1,500 pairs a day), and a much larger space than the forty-by-twenty-five-foot basement in which L.L. started making them, but the process is still virtually the same. And the boots are still made right here in Maine. Here's how:

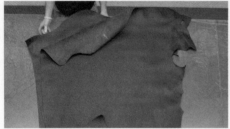

STEP 1: CUT LEATHER

Half-hides of whole-grain leather arrive at the 130,000-square-foot Bean manufacturing plant in Brunswick, Maine. Cutters work around tick bites, brands, and other imperfections for the best cuts. They place each cutting die down and hit the buttons, and the "clicker cutter" stamps out the shape, exerting 40,000 pounds of pressure. "Leather cutters hold a very important job in the factory," says Jack Samson, manager of manufacturing.

STEP 2: "SPLIT" PIECES

Stacks of leather parts, arranged by boot size, head for the "splitter," a machine that planes each piece to equal thickness and bevels its edges to prevent bunching or bulged seams that might chafe the boot's owner. Less-than-perfect sections of hide might be used for boot tongues, heel counters, or other out-of-sight parts. "Sixty-seven percent of the cost of the boot is in materials," says Samson.

STEP 3: STITCH PIECES

Sewers stitch together individual leather pieces. Air-cooled sewing machines whir at speeds up to 7,400 rpm. Machines might look new, but some date to the 1940s or earlier. Regular maintenance and rebuilding keeps the machines humming.

Top: L.L.Bean employees from past decades used nearly the same stitching technique as today's workers do.

STEP 4: PUNCH GROMMETS

The eyelet machine punches brass grommets into the leather upper at prescribed intervals. The Gumshoe version of the Bean Boot receives six eyelets; the sixteen-inch version gets twenty-eight eyelets.

STEP 5: SEW LINERS

In Gore-Tex® versions, liners are sewn to the upper. Every Gore-Tex liner is sealed with seam tape applied at 365° Fahrenheit, then submerged in a dip tank while pressurized. Any bubbles coming out lead to resealing until the liner is certified 100 percent air- (and therefore) watertight. Gore-Tex is one of several liner options, including Thinsulate™ and shearling.

STEP 6: MERGE TOPS AND BOTTOMS

Uppers unite with rubber bottoms. The bottoms are molded out of thermoplastic rubber at a Bean plant in Lewiston, Maine. A smear of cement applied to the rim of the bottom and double-sided tape on the upper keep the two pieces together temporarily.

STEP 7: SEW PIECES TOGETHER

A stitcher sews the boots with a triple-needled machine using waxed cotton thread. In L.L.'s day, stitchers made three passes with one needle. "Cotton thread swells when it gets wet, so it seals the holes," says Samson.

STEP 8: OUTPUT FINAL PRODUCT

Daily output of boots slows from 1,500 pairs to 1,200 when complicated versions of the Bean Boot, like the waxed canvas boot, are on the line. On a given day, the factory produces around twenty different styles of Bean boots; there are more than fifty possible styles to choose from.

STEP 9: SHIP TO CUSTOMER

Ready to rough it. Every boot bears a ticket generated by the Order Department that accompanies it through the factory. New bar coding will speed the process even more. Custom boots are direct-shipped right to the customer. Batch orders go to the company warehouse. Forty-five different workers have a hand in making the boots, with an average tenure on the factory floor of eighteen years. "Quality is impeccable and our reject rate is below one percent," says Samson.

might tumble. (The nearly identical Bean Boot, first issued in 1992, comes with a firmer, longer-wearing sole.) It certainly hasn't hurt that the boot's two-tone design holds timeless appeal.

The Hunting Shoe may appear outwardly unchanged by the passage of time, but beneath its leather-and-rubber exterior is a shoe remade and thoroughly updated. Begin with the rubber bottoms. In his day, L.L. shaped them from gum rubber and left them unlined. Today's Hunting Shoe is molded out of thermoplastic rubber, which offers superior crack and leak resistance. An integrated sock liner helps control the buildup of sweat. Customers can additionally choose from a variety of linings, including fleece, shearling, and Gore-Tex. On the early versions of the Maine Hunting Shoe, boot uppers were made of water-resistant elk calfskin, a kind of split leather. Today, the boot is sewn from full-grain cowhide that's specially tanned for extra water resistance. Gone is the optional metal-and-leather Maine Arched Innersole (83 cents postpaid) L.L. advertised for relief of "that flatfooted feeling." Instead, modern-era Maine Hunting Shoes gain torsional rigidity from a built-in steel shank and feature a foot-hugging inner sole for comfort underfoot.

Through the years and rounds of refinements, the Maine Hunting Shoe and Bean Boot have remained true to L.L.'s original designs, just as the company he created sticks to L.L.'s business method. Honest, straightforward, and enthusiastic, L.L. believed in fair dealing. He cultivated trust with his customers and suppliers. He had a saying that later became known as L.L.'s Golden Rule: "Sell good merchandise at reasonable profit, treat your customers like human beings, and they'll always come back for more." The ironclad L.L.Bean guarantee, first applied to the Maine Hunting Shoe and soon blanketing every product that L.L. sold, was an extension of that personal philosophy and a cornerstone of his company's success.

"Word-of-mouth advertising and customer satisfaction were critical to L.L.'s way of thinking," recalled Leon Gorman, L.L.'s grandson and the president of L.L.Bean from 1967 to 2001. "To hear that one of his products failed was a genuine shock to his system. He'd charge around the factory trying to find an explanation. Then he'd write the customer, return his money, enclose a gift, and invite him fishing or do anything to make the matter right. That customer was a real person to L.L., and he'd put his trust in L.L.'s catalog."

....

That sort of customer attention was a hit. As L.L.'s catalog, for which he wrote every word and supervised the layout himself, grew and gained wider circulation, people became curious about this mail-order mogul from Maine. Here's how a reporter for the *Lewiston Evening Journal* described L.L. in 1945: "Husky—he's a bit over 6 foot and works the scales in the 200 class— a voice that booms all over the place, a smile that is good natured and twinkling eyes which always glow in the fine appreciation of humor, L.L. is a typical out-of-doors man, the kind of a chap you'd know loved the woods and fields, the mountains, a sportsman."

Leon Leonwood Bean was born the fourth of six children to Benjamin and Sarah Bean of Greenwood, Maine, on October 13, 1872. His father, a farmer and carpenter, moved the family to Milton Plantation in the mountainous country near Bethel when L.L. was two. "My life up to the age of forty years was most uneventful, with a few exceptions," confessed L.L. After being orphaned at twelve, L.L., along with his younger brothers Ervin and Guy, was sent to live with a succession of family friends and relatives. A year later, L.L. shot his first deer on a hunting

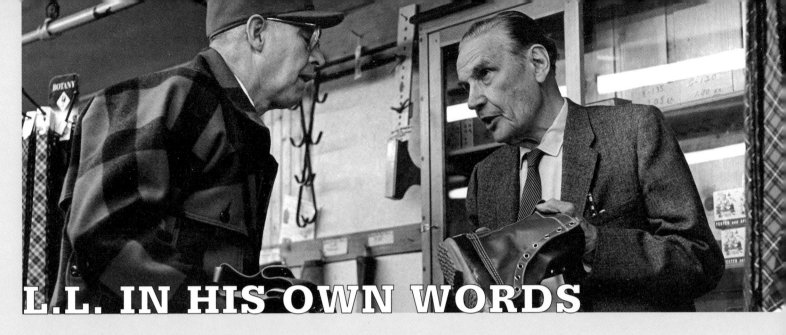

L.L. IN HIS OWN WORDS

HE WAS A PARAGON OF MAINELY VIRTUES, "ORACLE OF THE OUTDOORS," AND A FIRST-RATE SALESMAN. WHEN L.L. HAD SOMETHING ON HIS MIND (WHEN DIDN'T HE?), HE WAS HAPPY TO SHARE IT.

L.L. the Businessman

"Gosh, I like it! My job's not work! The days ain't long enough!"

"We increased our business only as fast as surplus profit would finance it. This may be a slow way, but it is certainly a safe way to finance any business."

"A customer is the most important person ever in the office...in person or by mail."

"Get their names!"

L.L. the Salesman

"I am very anxious that all my customers who do both duck hunting and stream fishing try a pair of these boots."

"I have personally used many rubber shirts but never saw the equal of this one for all around purposes.... Every fisherman should own one."

"I do not consider a sale complete until goods are worn out and customer still satisfied."

"This new practical up-to-date canoe is being offered for sale for the first time this season. From the day it was announced the demand has been so great that I could not resist listing it in my Spring Supplement."

L.L. the Thrifty Yankee

"We wish to call your attention to the fact that leather is so high that throwing away a pair of used sixteen-inch leather-top rubbers is about the same as throwing away a $5.00 bill."

"The success and pleasure of your outing depends largely on your equipment. You can easily spoil a wonderful trip by too much, too little, or not the right kind of an outfit.... Keep the weight and bulk down to comfortable necessities consistent with the means of transportation."

L.L. the Maine Guide

"Everyone is welcome to call for advice on where to hunt or fish and make a purchase if they see fit."

"A perfect trip may be ruined by one person who does not fit. I recommend small parties, not over four. Two makes a good party."

"You may fish all day and not get a strike. Therefore, make up your mind to have a good time. Enjoy camp life and exercise in the open air and you will be well repaid for your trip."

"In case one of your party does not show up at camp when night falls... do not get excited and do not do a thing until 6:00 P.M. If you start signaling before 6:00 P.M other hunters who have not gotten into camp are likely to butt in and make it very misleading."

"Do not shoot at anything until you are positive it is not a person. ALWAYS keep your safety on when in the company of another hunter."

THE BEAN CENTURY

Aha! Leon Leonwood Bean invents Maine Hunting Shoe

U.S. Postal Service adds parcel-post delivery

L.L. is first to send package from Freeport

L.L. patents key features on his hunting shoe

Employee #1: Hazel "Office Boss" Goldrup hired

Spanish-flu pandemic kills more Americans than WWI

1912

1917

1919

1911

1913

1918

L.L.'s mailer for novel hunting shoe earns one hundred orders.

Ninety pairs of L.L.'s boots returned for refund, imperiling his start-up

Women get their own version of Maine Hunting Shoe

U.S. enters World War I

Socks and such: Bean branches into apparel

Start of Prohibition

Waterproof Under-Pants appear in catalog and beneath wool pants

Bean ad placements cost $3,000; catalog printing reaches 35,000

The light weight friction lining makes them easy to dry as a dish. Just roll down the the leather tops, set them where it is warm and they are dry in ten minutes.

With every pair we give a small repair outfit that we warrant to mend a cut or snag in five minutes.

For all-round hunting purposes there is not a shoe on the market at any price equal to the Maine Hunting Shoe. See guarantee tag that is attached to every pair.

Price $3.50 delivered on approval anywhere in the U. S.

L. L. BEAN,
MANUFACTURER
FREEPORT, ME.

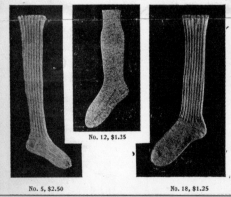

No. 12, $1.35

No. 5, $2.50

No. 18, $1.25

First wheels for L.L., a Reo

First-ever radio broadcast airs

L.L. purchases building where retail store now stands

Bean sales top $135,000; workforce hits twenty-five

Quirky L.L.Bean catalog judged best in the country

Soft sell: Camp Moccasin on sale

Babe Ruth, a big Bean fan, hits sixty dingers

1924

1926

1928

1920

1925

1927

Flapper dresses are all the rage

Added warmth: Hudson Bay Blanket debuts in catalog

Congress passes Air Commerce Act, licensing pilots and planes

Cars + camping = craze. Bean sleeping bag (at eleven pounds!) debuts

Flashlight, playing cards, and pocket watch offered for the complete camper

Hudson Bay Blankets
(Reg. U. S. Pat. Office No. 156544)

In the early days Indians traded furs for goods. The four marks shown on blanket indicated the price which was four large beaver skins. We also have 3½ point blankets that indicated a price of three large and one small beaver skins.

These blankets are so high grade and handsome that we cannot do them justice on paper.

We would like to send you one paying charges both ways, if you do not call it the best blanket you ever saw.

We have them in four colors: One 4 point, white with red, green, yellow and black stripes as shown. Three 3½ point, one red, one fawn and one white, each with one black stripe.

They are made of the very finest pure virgin wool, extra heavy and large with finished edges.

They are practically wind and water proof and will last a lifetime.

We consider them extra good values at the following prices:

4 point size 72" x 90" $16.50
3½ point size 66" x 84" $13.50
Delivered free in the U. S.

Vacationers have always been some of L.L.Bean's best customers. Opposite: Campers at Moosehead Lake, 1921. Left: Canoers in Great Pond, Belgrade, Maine, 1912.

trip with his cousin and constant companion on adventures, Louvie Swett. Not much went right—it took two shots using a balky borrowed rifle to bring down the small deer, L.L. had to abandon the dressed carcass due to darkness, and dragging the deer into camp the next morning was exhausting—but a lifelong passion was born.

John Gould, a longtime columnist for the *Christian Science Monitor* and fellow Freeporter, knew L.L. from childhood as the fellow who loaned him a rifle for his first hunting trip. "Mr. Bean has a native reluctance toward hyperbole, and is more inclined to tell you what he did than the kind of fellow he is," wrote Gould. "Yet there never existed a more colorful man, and in Freeport, where characters have always been a dime a dozen, he stands out."

Gould liked to tell an amusing tale of a hard-of-hearing L.L. in later years. "Mr. Bean always had a booming, resonant voice, and as with most who begin to hear poorly he grew in the habit of shouting, as if that cleared things up all around," he recalled. "As a consequence, any business

conversation Mr. Bean had [over the telephone] was heard resounding up and down Freeport like a shotgun blast." It so happened that L.L.'s stockbroker called every morning to discuss investments, their conversation ending with L.L shouting out to buy and sell orders. "About half the mature male population of Freeport would contrive to be on the post office steps when the broker called. As every word spoken was clearly articulate on the street below, there developed in Freeport a knowing set of investors who would soon disperse to call their own brokers," wrote Gould.

L.L.'s mail-order business flourished through the 1920s as he expanded his catalog lineup to include fishing and hunting gear and apparel, snowshoes, and variations on the Maine Hunting Shoe such as the Maine Guide Shoe and Maine Cruising Shoe, as well as lifestyle products like horseshoes ("Put a pair near your camp or cottage and note how quickly your place becomes popular") and the Hudson Bay Blanket.

In no small part, Bean's good fortune was owed to his catalog's reception among out-

THE MAINE MYSTIQUE

MIX TWO PARTS REALITY WITH ONE PART FANTASY TO REACH THE PERFECT STATE.

Think of Maine and you think lobster, moose, and L.L.Bean, and not necessarily in that order. So entwined is the company with the image of the state that former governor John McKernan once quipped, "Is Maine Maine because of Bean, or is Bean Bean because of Maine?"

To fully comprehend the phenomenon of L.L.Bean, it's useful to know something about the company's base of operation. To begin with, Maine is really two states. There's the actual place, a rough and forested land inhabited by famously terse and independent-minded sorts. And then there's Maine the state of mind, an invention with shared ownership between Mainers and the out-of-staters who love it. L.L.'s genius fused both states.

A lot about Maine can be explained by its isolation. Stuck in a far corner of the country and guarded by ocean, big rivers, tangled forest, and craggy mountains, Maine was for the better part of its history very difficult to reach. It took Teddy Roosevelt several days to get there from New York by ship, train, and buggy as a callow youth in need of toughening. That isolation, combined with a harsh climate and thin, rocky soil, allowed the undiluted development of a definable character, a way of life, and a wicked good accent.

"The people who founded Maine were involved in fishing, forestry, and farming," says Angus King, governor of Maine from 1995 to 2003. "Those three pursuits are all independent, do-it-yourself kinds of businesses. You go out in the woods with an ax, go out on the ocean in a boat, you plow the field. That's a piece in developing this flinty, New England self-reliance."

Mainers enjoy a reputation for uprightness. (L.L. Bean, the man, was no exception.) As a practical matter, doing business with honesty and integrity is the only way to make it in a sparsely populated state that's still like "a big small town," as Governor King puts it. "If repeat business is all there is—like running a little restaurant in Houlton—you'd better be honest or they aren't coming back," he says.

Donald A. Wilson, who grew up in Maine and has written nine books about places and people from the state's past, including *Silver Trout and Moonlight: Stories of Mack Brown, Maine Guide,* is a close observer of Homo Mainus. "Maine people are very independent, well informed, but don't want anyone messing around with their way of life or trying to influence the way they think," he says.

Then there's Mainers' legendary coolness with strangers, which Dean Bennett, professor emeritus at the University of Maine at Farmington and author of *Nature and Renewal: Wild River Valley and Beyond,* explains. "We're somewhat socially wary until we get a feel for what a person is like. But once accepted you're received exceptionally warmly," he says.

Gaining that acceptance can take a while, if for no other reason than that the withholding is such good sport. "My tombstone will say, 'He did all right for a boy from away,'" says Governor King, a native of Virginia who moved to Maine nearly fifty years ago. "My oldest boy was born in Skowhegan, Maine, in 1970, and I ran into this old farmer I knew up on Water Street. I was all excited, and I said, 'Mr. Forbis, guess what? I just had a son born in the Skowhegan Hospital. He's a native of Maine!' The old man looked at me over his glasses and said, 'Well, by gahry, just 'cause the cat has her kittens in the oven, don't make 'em biscuits.'"

Geography shaped Maine's destiny, and it has also proved an irresistible lure to outsiders. Until Willis Carrier patented his "Apparatus for Treating Air" in 1906, Maine was air-conditioning. Families of means decamped to Maine for the entire summer to escape the heat, their letters home inspiring the perspiring to follow suit. Abundant deer, Atlantic salmon, and brook trout drew hunters and anglers, who returned with tall tales of the great North Woods.

In the crowded East, Maine stands in for the final frontier, a psychic assurance that the last good place still exists. And why not? Sections of the state that are bigger than Rhode Island have no paved roads or incorporated towns, and moose outnumber humans. Wherever a flatlander is from, in his mind Maine is certain to be cooler, purer, and wilder. With reports of mountain lions and eastern timber wolves reclaiming their rightful territory in the North Woods, and the state more heavily forested today than in L.L.'s time, Maine, if anything, is becoming even wilder.

The perception of Maine as a bastion of wilderness and old ways ranges far. Donald Wilson recalls a conversation with a guide he hired while in primeval Alaska. "Maine, huh? That's got to be the last big woods," said the guide. "I'd like to get there someday."

1926 SPRING SUPPLEMENT

L. L. Bean, Manufacturer
FREEPORT, MAINE

1928 Fall CATALOG
L.L.BEAN
MFGR.
FREEPORT MAINE

Clockwise from above: Spring 1926 supplement; fall 1928 catalog; Eighth-, quarter-, and full-pint cans of Bean's Water-Proof Dressing, for treating boot leather. Opposite: Fall 1929 catalog.

of-state hunters, fisherman, and people who vacationed in Maine each year. The style of vacationing in the outdoors was very different in those days before widespread automobile ownership and good-quality roads penetrated the state's hinterlands. Entire families would travel by railroad to such full-service sporting camps as Mt. Kineo House and William Tell Hunting Club on Moosehead Lake, or Buckhorn Camps near Millinocket. Anglers and hunters were always accompanied by a knowledgeable guide who knew where the fish and game could be found and, equally important, knew the boundaries of Maine's complicated patchwork of private holdings. Vacations lasted for weeks, as families sought escape from the summer heat back home in Boston, New York, or Philadelphia. A trip north couldn't be contemplated without first ordering necessities out of Mr. Bean's catalog.

The demands of operating his business consumed more and more of his time, but L.L. remained at heart an outdoorsman and enthusiastic believer in the health-promoting benefits of outdoor living. "He saw a greater good in the outdoors business than simply selling products by mail," said Gorman. "L.L. was not one to philosophize a lot or pontificate, but he had a personal relationship with the great outdoors. It was there that people were at their best, he believed, and his quintessential products, like the Maine Hunting Shoe, helped their users go outdoors and reap the benefits of being there."

The small start-up by the penniless orphan from rural Maine found its legs in the 1920s: sales passed the $100,000 mark, catalogs were regularly shipped to every continent, and its Maine Hunting Shoe won praise from Arctic explorer Admiral D.B. MacMillan and the men on his expeditions. So far, so good, but as the 1929 stock-market crash loomed, it was anyone's guess how a company based on leisure pursuits would ride out the worst economic downturn in the nation's history.

1929 Catalog
FALL
L.L.BEAN
FREEPORT MAINE

CHAPTER 2

DURABLE GOODS FOR TOUGH TIMES

The **CHAMOIS CLOTH SHIRT**

First sold in **1927**

THE CHAMOIS CLOTH SHIRT PROMISED WARMTH, COMFORT, AND DURABILITY—QUALITIES THAT ENSURED SALES EVEN DURING THE GREAT DEPRESSION. AS COMPETITORS WENT BELLY-UP, L.L.BEAN QUADRUPLED ITS REVENUE, SELLING A GROWING RANGE OF PRODUCTS THAT L.L. OFTEN FIELD-TESTED HIMSELF. PART OF IT WAS GOOD TIMING. WORKERS LUCKY ENOUGH TO AVOID UNEMPLOYMENT FOUND THEM-SELVES WITH PAID VACATION, AND AS MIDDLE-CLASS FAMILIES TOOK TO THE WILDERNESS, L.L.BEAN SUPPLIED THE GEAR FOR THEIR ADVENTURES.

Styles come and styles go. Then there's the Chamois Cloth Shirt. The shirt is soft, but it's tough as nails. David Penley, a nine-year veteran of working the L.L.Bean retail store during the graveyard shift, tells of the night a man in his eighties came in clutching a Chamois Shirt that looked as old as its owner. "The collar was frayed, and the rest of the shirt was so worn the nap was completely gone. I figured he was heading to Returns," says David. "Instead, he says, 'This is a good shirt. I'll take another one.'"

Introduced to the L.L.Bean catalog in 1927, this rugged and warm cotton shirt quickly became a perennial customer favorite and has appeared every year since. The shirt's appeal today is the same as when L.L. touted the shirt in the Spring 1933 catalog: "Absolutely will not shrink and is more durable than wool," he wrote. "The longer it is worn the more it feels and looks like chamois leather." Indeed, more Chamois Cloth Shirts were sold in 2011 than at any point in the garment's lengthy history.

During its eighty-four years of uninterrupted production, the only substantial thing changed about the Chamois Cloth Shirt is the name. L.L. first tagged it as the Leatherette Shirt because of its likeness to high-grade chamois leather, the kind used in buckskin shirts and lederhosen. Four years later the shirt took on the name we know it by to this day. "It's a piece of wearable Americana," says Don Rogers, product line manager for men's apparel at L.L.Bean.

At the root of the Chamois Shirt's staying power lie the softness and "hand" of its 7.5-ounce Portuguese flannel. Making chamois involves passing cotton fabric beneath rotating drums equipped with metal brushes that raise a nap or fuzz. It's a fine line between a chamois that feels soft and luxurious and one so thick that it pills unattractively. "Brushing woven cotton is a blending of art and science," says Rogers. "Old world handling by our vendor in Portugal raises the 'peach' of the cloth on both sides for warmth and comfort. That's the magic."

L.L. intended the Chamois Cloth Shirt for use on hunting and fishing trips. Gentlemen of his era wore it tucked in as a heavy shirt, although today it is perfectly acceptable to wear pulled out as a light jacket over another shirt. Over the years, the shirt has been variously promoted in the catalog for being "wind resistant," "warm and durable as wool," and "very soft and comfortable to wear." L.L. knew he had a winner based on sales reports for the Chamois Shirt, but today, real-time customer reviews on the L.L.Bean web-site say it directly: "super shirt," "best shirt ever!" and "love the shirt." On a scale of five, customers rate the Chamois Cloth Shirt a 4.8, placing it among the highest-rated of any Bean product.

For its first three decades, the shirt was available in exactly one color: tan. In 1960 bright red was introduced. "The scarlet is a good fishing shirt

Bean's Chamois Cloth Shirts
(For Men, Women and Children)

This is the shirt Mr. Bean used on his hunting and fishing trips. It has been in our line since 1927 and gets more popular each year.

Chamois Cloth fabric is fine grade 7 oz. cotton flannel, thickly napped on both sides. Wind-resistant, warm and durable, it is very soft and comfortable to wear.

Made on extra full shirt patterns; with two large breast pockets with button flaps, long sleeves and long tuck-in tails. (Women's model has squared tails.) Well made with placket front, placketed sleeve openings and strong double-needle stitching on side seams, armholes and sleeves. Machine Wash.

Six colors: Green. Bright Red. Navy. Ivory. Tan. Slate Blue.
Men's Regular sizes: 14½ to 20. Wt. 17 oz.
1611P Men's Regular Chamois Cloth Shirt, $19.00 ppd.

Men's Long sizes: 15 to 19. Wt. 19 oz.
1612P Men's Long Chamois Cloth Shirt, $20.00 ppd.

Women's sizes: 6 to 20. Wt. 14 oz.
4311P Women's Chamois Cloth Shirt, $19.00 ppd.

Children's sizes: 8 to 18. Wt. 10 oz.
Five colors: Navy. Bright Red. Tan. Slate Blue. Green.
4335P Children's Chamois Cloth Shirt, $17.50 ppd.

Above: The Chamois Shirt as advertised in 1983. Right: Rock Hudson dons a classic L.L.Bean Shirt in 1955. Opposite: The Chamois Shirt makes its debut as the "Leather-ette."

Maine Outing Shirt

Is the very best, fine, all wool shirt that can be made. They are roomy and long, tailored and trimmed to suit the most particular.

Be sure and send for free samples of these shirts as we cannot do them justice on paper.

Four patterns: Two checks as shown at left. Two plain, one dark tan and one light fawn.

All very neat patterns for summer wear.

Sizes; 14½ to 19.

Price, $5.50, delivered free in the United States.

Bean's Leatherette Shirt

I have personally been testing this Shirt on my hunting and fishing trips for over two years and prefer it to any woolen shirt ever tried.

The fabric will not shrink and is much more durable than woolen.

Closed front only.

Color; Olive Drab.

Send for free sample.

Sizes; 14½ to 19.

Price, $4.00. Postpaid.

Bean's Summer Outing Shirt

Is made of 50% light gray wool that will not shrink. A very full sized shirt with two breast pockets as shown.

This is the neatest and best summer shirt, for the price, we have ever offered.

Sizes; 14½ to 19.

Price; $2.85. Postpaid.

$6.50

Bean's Wool Camp Blouse

This is an all wool Blouse that has proved to be one of the most popular garments we have ever offered. It is a very practical, medium weight, sporty looking, up-to-date Blouse.

The knit bottom allows it to be worn outside the pants as a sweater or inside as a shirt.

Color; Dark Tan with Orange overplaid.

As we cannot do this garment justice on paper, we would like to send you one. You can return it and we will not only refund your money, but pay postage both ways should it not suit you.

Price; $6.50. Postpaid. Send for free sample of cloth.

as red repels black flies. Also safe for dragging in deer without coat," claimed a catalog from that era. By 1982 the shirt was available in six colors: tan, bright red, navy, green, slate blue, and ivory. After that came a deluge of hues, each year's selection providing a snapshot of prevailing color trends. In the mid-1980s, bright colors like light turquoise, teal, and emerald green were the thing. Today earth tones dominate, with burgundy, navy, and hunter being the biggest sellers.

An enduring mystery surrounding the Chamois Cloth Shirt is the purpose behind its distinctive angled-flap button pockets. Are they there so when you raise your rifle, the gunstock won't catch on the pocket? Or so when you're bent over installing hardwood flooring (L.L.'s dad was a carpenter), you can slip your pencil in and it won't fall out? "We have many theories," notes Don Rogers. "We know there was a functional reason for the angled pocket—L.L.Bean has always been a problem-solving company—but what that was is lost to time."

....

Robust sales for the newly introduced Chamois Shirt and the overall vibrant health of L.L.Bean's mail-order business stood in sharp contrast to what was going on everywhere else in America. The Great Depression was hitting its full, ruinous stride. Jobs were scarce, banks were closing, stocks had tanked, and American families had to pinch their pennies hard. Companies too numerous to count simply vanished. Yet up in Freeport, L.L. was drawing plans to double the size of his factory in 1932. "The plant was too small,

BEAN BY THE NUMBERS

Shoe size of giant Bean Boot at retail store entrance:

410

Highest single-day call volume (2010):

119,000

Record for single-day web orders (2010):

127,000+

Packages shipped annually:

13,000,000

Daily Bean Boot output at Brunswick, Maine factory:

1,500

Miles walked daily by product picker at Bean warehouse:

8

Annual visits to Bean stores in Freeport:

3,000,000

Increase in 2011 Bean Boot sales over prior year:

57%

Free cups of coffee dispensed at flagship store overnight:

125

Price of ten-inch Maine Hunting Shoe, 1921:

$8.00

Price of ten-inch Maine Hunting Shoe, 2012:

$109.00

Size of the biggest trout in the retail store aquarium:

8 pounds, 28 inches

New addition to our Factory

Three stories, 90 by 100 feet, will be completed October 1st, 1941. To our loyal customers we are indebted for our ability to expand.

L. L. Bean, Pres.

much too small," wrote L.L. in *My Story*, "and an efficiency man chuckled at the manufacturing procedures which can be explained only by this fact; the business had grown so fast that I had time only for filling orders and let the methods take care of themselves."

L.L.Bean didn't merely survive the worst economic conditions in modern history; it boomed. Company revenue quadrupled during the Depression decade to more than $1 million. Optimism was in short supply in most places, but the mail-order mogul of Maine brimmed with it. "Our business for the year ending July 1, 1935, showed an increase of 29 percent over the previous year. We have just broken ground for a large addition that will be shown in our 1936 fall catalog," boasted L.L. on the editorial page of the 1935 Bean catalog.

How did L.L.Bean thrive as scores of other retailers withered? Durable goods, a great reputation, and savvy retailing had a lot to do with it. But America was also changing in ways that played to L.L.Bean's strengths. Paid vacation, a foreign concept during the industrial era, was becoming the norm (for those lucky enough to be working). By the end of the 1930s, half of

L. L. Bean's Business Has Had A Phenomenal Growth

Freeport's Huge Mail Order House Is A Monument To The Ingenuity And Progressiveness Of Its Founder And Owner

In the space of twenty years L. L. Bean of Freeport has seen his business rise from a new shoe that he designed and had made for his own personal use to a tremendous mail order house whose catalogs go to every nation on earth.

L. L. Bean has just opened his new factory for the expected increase in his fall business, and has just issued a 52 page catalog that lists the many things he sells today. Because of this it is interesting to trace his truly phenomenal rise in the business world, a rise that Freeport people know well enough, and which most of them have watched.

office and the shipping room drop directly onto the sorting tables. Last year L. L. Bean's postage bill was $25,021.35—or 74% of the total business of the post office in the fiscal year ending July 1. During a part of the year the Bean mail puts the post office into a first class office position, but of course Bean's business is seasonal, and during his slack time the average falls off. Freeport, at times, does more post office business than Brunswick—solely because of Bean's factory.

The factory is a curious place, because of the variety of goods made. For example, a couple of boys who

L. L. Bean's factory in Freeport, showing the addition that has just been opened for the coming fall business.

Opposite: Stock room in the L.L.Bean retail store, 1936. Employee Walter "Tubby" Colbath sits at right. Top left: Editor's note in catalog, 1941. Above: The *Brunswick Record*, Thursday, August 23, 1934.

L.L. Bean Inc.
Freeport. Maine

Dear Friends:
　　Just a note to accompany my
orders for a new pair of cold weather boots.
The last pair saved me from loosing
my left foot. I got it caught in
the track (between belt & motor
driven wheel) of a Snow-machine
and my arch was crunched & broken
badly but if it hadn't been for
my Bean Boot & Liner I would
have lost my foot! It tore up
the rubber completely across the
instep & side. I am grateful for
your sturdy products & await
my new pair of boots.
　　　　　　Yours truly,
　　　　　　　　Bonnie M.

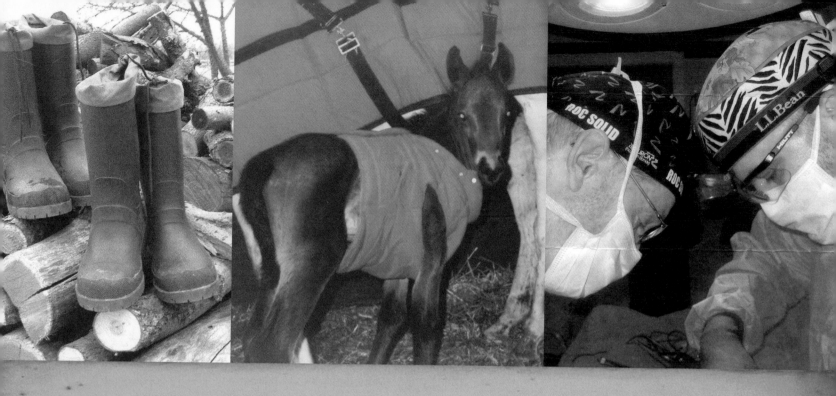

100 YEARS OF SAVING THE DAY

OCCASIONALLY, BEAN'S STURDY AND RELIABLE PRODUCTS PLAY
VITAL ROLES IN UNEXPECTED SITUATIONS.

"Recently a car slid off the road near our house into icy, flooded river water. The temperature outside was 13 degrees, the wind howling at 25 mph. All the members of my family who went to the rescue were wearing these boots by Bean. Even after several hours in these weather conditions, an hour or more of which we were submerged in 12 inches of ice-encrusted water, our feet stayed toasty warm and dry.

P.S. The driver was cold and scared but fine."

—G.W., Upper Sandusky, Ohio, January 21, 2004

"As you can see by the enclosed photographs, my L.L.Bean vest kept an early 1981 thoroughbred filly toasty warm on a record-cold Alabama night. In the pictures, she is only hours old. After three days of "baby wear," enough time for her to get fuzzy, I reclaimed my vest, washed it, and am still wearing it! Our filly sends her thanks—as she gallops in our lovely springtime weather!"

—Dana P., Leeds, Alabama, March 13, 1981

"I recently returned from a medical mission in Hyderabad, India, where we performed over 150 various surgeries in about ten days. We did not know what kind of equipment we would find at the local hospital where we worked. As one could imagine, lighting is a crucial part of surgery. The lights they provided were in poor condition and not very substantial. The picture enclosed shows two of the surgeons from our group providing a thyroidectomy. As you can see, my L.L.Bean headlight provided the much-needed extra lighting to get the job done. You probably would not have imagined that your products have now moved from camping and recreation to the surgical area!"

—Jerry F., West Bloomfield, Michigan, February 4, 2008

Bean's Pine Tree Poleless Tent

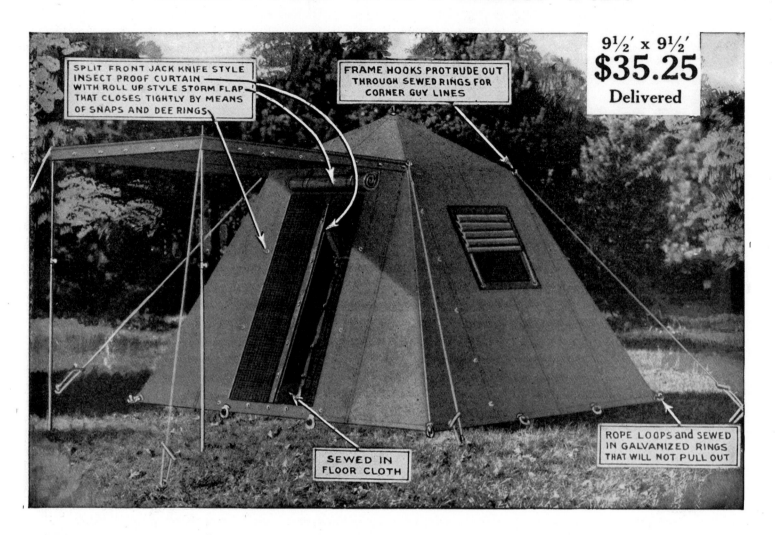

9½' x 9½'
$35.25
Delivered

SPLIT FRONT JACK KNIFE STYLE INSECT PROOF CURTAIN WITH ROLL UP STYLE STORM FLAP THAT CLOSES TIGHTLY BY MEANS OF SNAPS AND DEE RINGS

FRAME HOOKS PROTRUDE OUT THROUGH SEWED RINGS FOR CORNER GUY LINES

SEWED IN FLOOR CLOTH

ROPE LOOPS and SEWED IN GALVANIZED RINGS THAT WILL NOT PULL OUT

After experimenting with dozens of different tents, we have decided on the above Poleless Umbrella Tent as the best and most practical for auto camping that can be made regardless of price. In testing a large number of tents we have picked the good and discarded the bad features.

1st. The Umbrella Tent with sewed in floor, for auto camping, has proven beyond doubt its superiority over all other types of tents.

2nd. Material is new light weight, dry finish, dark olive green, 12 ounce duck that is waterproof and mildewproof. It is fast color and will not smut. A handsome tent that will not show dirt.

3rd. Size 9½' x 9½'. Floor space of 90 sq. ft. Cannot be beaten for all-around camping purposes. It is a comfortable four party tent and with awning curtains and auto-bed, will accommodate six. A smaller tent is not large enough and a larger tent is too heavy to handle.

4th. Frame, without centre-pole, as shown, is by far the most practical we have ever seen. No complicated or tricky adjustments. One person can easily erect in six minutes. Adjustments for tautness and uneven ground quickly made by handy self-acting patented clamps (see cut opposite page) on telescoping corner poles. (Continued on next page.)

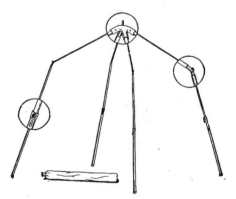

New Light Weight Adjustable Steel Tubing Frame

Camping

The great demand for auto camping equipment has flooded the market with a bewildering mixture of Tents and other articles that make it hard for a camper to decide just what is needed.

For nearly two years we have been testing and examining Tents and other camping equipment.

As a result dozens of Tents and other articles have been discarded.

In selecting the following items we are not trying to see how much we can sell, but instead to cut down to the bare necessities in order to protect our customers against wasting one dollar on unnecessary equipment.

All our camping goods are delivered free anywhere in the United States east of the Mississippi.

liberating, "auto camping" was the rage, and L.L. fine-tuned his catalog to meet the needs of the "tin can tourist."

....

L.L.'s selection process for new items for his catalog was not based on market surveys or merchandising analyses. He simply went with his gut and his personal experience. If he approved of a product on one of his hunting and fishing trips, it stood a good chance of getting in. Sometimes a product was developed in-house and then field-tested until the kinks were worked out. Other times, as with the Hudson Bay Blanket, he simply offered another manufacturer's product. The particulars behind L.L.'s decisions on product placement in the early years are generally unknown. He wasn't much for record-keeping and was even less inclined toward noting his thoughts on paper. Despite being such an outgoing public figure, to

American workers would earn paid time off, the luckiest enjoying two weeks or more. Whereas a Sunday afternoon spent picnicking in a local park was the best the average person could muster at the turn of the twentieth century, Americans in the late 1930s had sufficient time off to travel out of town. And with a shiny Buick or Ford in the driveway, they now had the means.

Throughout the Victorian era and into the early decades of the twentieth century, vacationing was a distinctly upper-class pursuit. While the masses sweltered through the summer months in the inner city, high society retired to resorts and grand hotels at White Sulphur Springs, West Virginia; Saratoga Springs, New York; Mackinac Island, Michigan; and the like. Had they the money to stay in such luxury, it's doubtful the new breed of footloose wage earners would have been welcome. Instead, America's middle class took to the road. With practically no tourist infrastructure of inexpensive hotels or motels in existence, vacation destinations were limited. Out of necessity, leisure travelers took to tenting. To these freewheelers, it didn't much matter whether the ideal camping spot was in a national park or a farmer's field as long as it was far from the crowded, noisy city. Inexpensive and

Opposite: 1932 advertisement for the poleless tent. Above left: A 1927 statement of Bean's camping philosphy. Below: Tin mug from pre-1920.

STORE PAID THE BILLS, BUT L.L. LIVED FOR
TRIPS UP NORTH EVERY AUTUMN.

PUSHING THE EDGE

Innovation runs in the DNA at Bean. It started with L.L. marrying rubber boots to leather hikers to create the Maine Hunting Shoe and continues through today. Here, recent break-throughs pioneered by L.L.Bean:

Polartec Windbloc (1992)
Bean collaborated with Malden Mills to introduce a fleece material with a polyurethane membrane barrier that repels wind and water.

PrimaLoft (1993)
In partnership with Albany International, Bean gave this lightweight, synthetic insulation its first commercial application in jackets and parkas.

Aqua Stealth Wading Shoe (1996)
Sticky rubber soles on the wading shoes reduce the transfer of invasive species from watershed to watershed while still keeping anglers upright.

Helix Waders (2008)
Problem: Darts sewn into wader knees for ease of movement create weak links against water intrusion. Solution: A spiraling seam running up each leg that cuts overall seams by half.

Waterproof Sling Pack (2009)
Getting at pack contents while fishing in waist-deep water usually requires a third hand to hold the rod. The Sling Pack's single bandolier strap allows the wearer to pivot the pack from back to chest one-handed.

this day he engenders some degree of mystery. Much of what we do know about him is reflected in oral histories and accounts kept by the people who worked or hunted with him. Justin Williams, a longtime Bean employee in the early days, provided such a mirror. His recollection of a particular duck-hunting trip in the late 1930s gives us a glimpse of product development, L.L.-style:

"I had this old duck call that I got around 1938 or so—one of the best ever made," said Williams. "L.L. and Danny Snow were in one blind and I was in another with the dog. So I got this old duck call out and used it. Within a few minutes there must have been 500 ducks flying around the blinds. I mean the sky was filled with ducks. L.L. was standing there in shock, and till the day he died, he never got over it. You can believe that the next fall he had duck calls in his catalog…patterned after the one I used that day."

Williams also witnessed what happened when one of L.L.'s field tests went awry. In this case, L.L. was trying out a fancy new fishing rod that had been pressed on him by a salesman for possible inclusion in the catalog. The fact that several other outfitters had placed big orders for the rod didn't impress L.L. "He took the rod on a fishing trip, hooked onto a big fish, the rod snapped in half and went overboard. That was the end of that," said Williams.

"It wasn't easy to sell to L.L.," recalled Williams. "He had to see the truth of things for himself. If he put a product in the catalog,

Pages 48-49: From left to right, Dr. Arthur Gould, Walter Dumser, Charlie Manchester, and L.L. camping near Sebago Lake, circa 1940. Above: Fall catalog with the State of Maine blanket. Opposite, top: L.L.Bean employee picnic, Freeport, August 24, 1939. Opposite, bottom: During a summer 1939 fishing party at Moosehead Lake, L.L. was joined (from his right) by Gould, Willis Libby, and Levi Patterson.

THE FACE OF BEAN: GEORGE SOULE

When it came to outsmarting waterfowl in the middle decades of the last century, you wanted George Soule on your side. Or least a passel of Soule's exquisitely carved and lifelike duck decoys. L.L. Bean always ventured out with both.

"George, let's you and I go duck-hunting—don't bother to punch out," L.L. was known to say to his shipping clerk during duck season in the 1930s. Soule also oversaw Bean's fly-tying operation, which employed sixteen nimble-fingered women at its peak. Forty years of age separated the mail-order magnate and the young Freeporter with the penchant for wood carving, but there was no duck-hunting companion L.L. would rather have than Soule.

Duck decoys were fairly primitive at the time. Until 1935, when the practice was finally outlawed in Maine, live ducks were used to lure other ducks. Soule didn't care much for L.L.'s artificial ducks. "Hell, I could whittle a better-looking bunch of decoys than that mess we're using," he said.

"Then do it," replied L.L.

In no time, Soule was up and running independently with Maine Coastal Decoys. In a good year his company turned out more than fifteen thousand ducks and geese, a third of which were sold through the Bean catalog. His decoys were renowned for having a swiveling head that assumed natural poses.

"Soule has probably done more to assist the modern duck hunter than anyone else," wrote *Sports Afield* magazine in 1974. "The excellence of his decoy has become the standard against which other commercial duck decoys are compared."

When the market for his oversize hunting decoys slowed in the 1970s, Soule enjoyed great success selling hand-painted decorative decoys through the Bean catalog. He died in 1997. A one-hundreth-anniversary limited-edition pair of Soule's stand-up black ducks will be available at llbean.com in fall 2012.

Opposite: George Soule at work in the Fly Tying Department, 1935. Above: Mallard-drake decoy with removable head, circa 1940s.

MIDNIGHT RUN

Keep the doors open 24/7/365, as Bean has done at its flagship store since 1951, and you never know who or what will walk in during the night. The current sales team on the midnight-to-8 a.m. shift recollects some more memorable encounters.

KELLY MCKELLOR, TEN-YEAR VETERAN:

Heavy-metal band **Korn.** "Stocking up on winter gear for their tour in Moscow."

John Travolta. "Haven't seen him in a few years."

Rambunctious grads: "Falmouth High kids on graduation night trying on everything, running everywhere."

Taylor Swift and her mom. "We've also had country singers Brooks & Dunn, Amy Grant, and Vince Gill, and members of Blink 182."

Fire in a fitting room. "A member of security grabbed an extinguisher and was able to limit the burn area—and keep the sprinklers from activating."

DAVID PENLEY, NINE-YEAR VETERAN:

Snorer. "Guy was sound asleep in a tent. I let him sleep until 6 a.m."

A cappella singing. "Tufts University's group The Beelzebubs make coming to the store part of their initiation."

Streaker. "She wasn't exactly young and slender."

Pinpoint purchasing. "College frats require a cash-register receipt from our store stamped at exactly 3:31 a.m. or 4:31 a.m. So kids hang around the counter and shout, 'I gotta buy this. Now!'"

you can bet it was tested and was worth having, and no doubt about it at all. He started building a reputation for that right from the beginning."

By 1934 the L.L.Bean catalog had expanded to fifty-two pages and was mailed twice yearly to more than 100,000 people. The mailing list would reach nearly 300,000 names by decade's end. For many, the arrival of the catalog in the mailbox was an eagerly anticipated event, a form of visual entertainment before televisions and computers were common in American households. "The day the L.L.Bean catalogues arrive, there is no work done in the office of any New England sportsman," wrote Dorothy Gulick in *Yankee* magazine in 1940. A helpless big-game hunter wrote to L.L.: "Your catalog is a dangerous book. A sportsman can no more pass it up than a drunkard can pass up a saloon."

From camp slippers to a "pole-less" tent, an air mattress, and a nine-inch trout knife, Bean's comprehensive inventory could satisfy a camper and hunter's every need—as well as those of daydreamers. Popular product introductions during the 1930s included the Blucher Moccasin, the Double L Bamboo Rod, Brook

SPRING 1935

FREE CATALOG
Just Off the Press

Fully illustrated, showing footwear, clothing, and other specialties for Fisherman and Camper.

L. L. BEAN, Inc.
49 Main Street, Freeport, Maine

Trout Flies, the Business Man's Shirt, and the Sportsman's Kit Bag. Customers bought these items with confidence, even from thousands of miles away, because they saw L.L. Bean as an ethical man doing business the right way. "I personally test out practically all of our new specialties before offering them for sale," he assured everyone in his catalog. For most, that was convincing enough.

As the catalog grew, people began taking an interest in the wavy-haired, bow-tie-wearing gentleman so confident in his

Above: An advertisement in *National Geographic* magazine for the spring 1935 Bean catalog. Opposite: Bean fan Alvin Pringle receives his spring 1943 catalog.

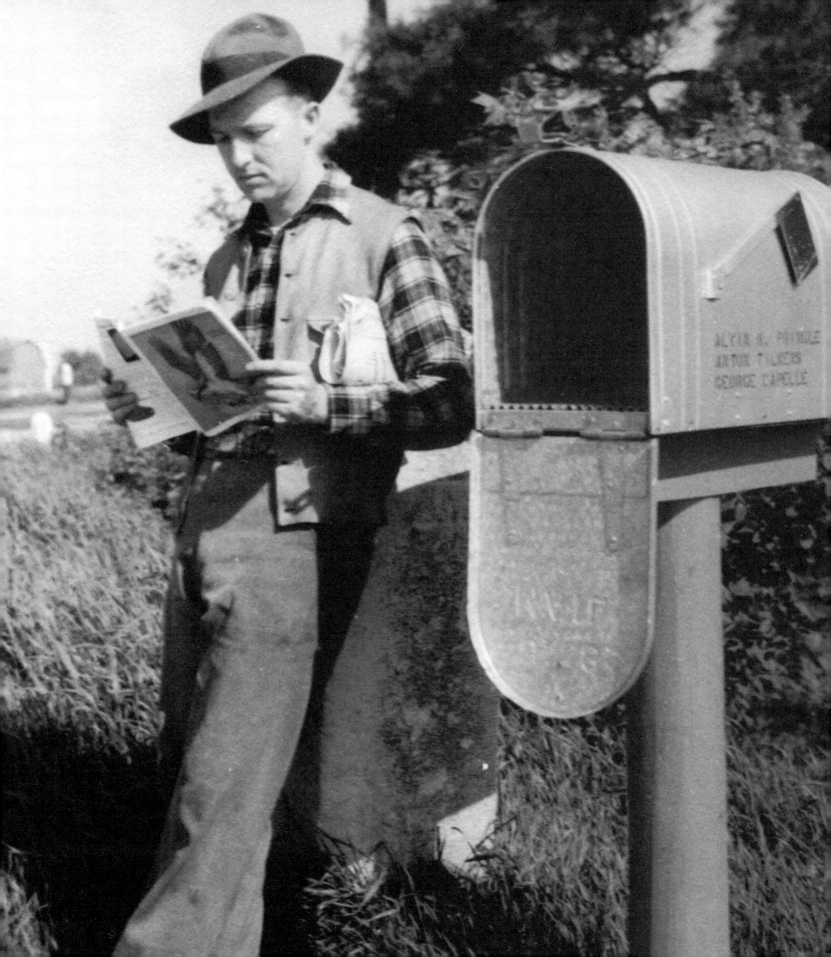

A BEAN IN EVERY MAILBOX

SPRING 1938

L.L.BEAN Inc.

MANUFACTURER
FREEPORT
MAINE

L.L.Bean began with L.L.'s direct-mail piece announcing his Maine Hunting Shoes. Just over a decade later, his circulars became a real catalog, and a tradition was born. L.L. wrote the copy himself in his direct, sincere voice and selected all the products. Streaked with hand-drawn printer's rules and surprising pairings—stockings and a fishing bag for instance—the contents focused less on design than on promoting guaranteed quality. Pages weren't ready for the press until they received L.L.'s official "OK" (see red stamps, opposite). Under Leon Gorman's direction in the 1960s, the catalog was given a neater appearance, but to this day its aura remains quintessentially Bean.

Opposite, clockwise from top left: Catalog pages from 1936 (Trouting Boot); 1930 (Hunting Coat); 1943 (page with L.L.'s "OK" stamps); 2011 (Pet Cuddler); 1961 (Flashlight and telephone number); 2011 (Slippers); 1957 (Maple Syrup and Pocket Watch); 1977 (Flannel Sheets); 1972 (Bandanna Shirt); and 1943 (Ration Book Case).

Bean's Tan Trouting Boot

$6.85

Made of dark tan rubber twice as tough as that used in ordinary boots. Color, which is compounded especially for us, makes boots practically invisible when wading or duck hunting.

It is the lightest wading boot made, comes almost to the waist and when rolled down will go in coat pocket.

A new feature is cleated sole as shown. A distinct help in preventing slipping while tramping or wading.

Perfectly adapted for stream fishing, duck hunting, washing car, swamp hunting, and general dull weather outing. Very easy to dry out, as tops can be rolled way down. Can fit all feet from A to EE.

With every pair we give a small repair outfit that will mend a snag or cut in three minutes. Send for free sample of rubber and try to puncture it with stick or pencil.

We have this boot in both Men's and Ladies.'

Price: Men's sizes 5 to 12, $6.85. Ladies' sizes 3 to 8, $5.85.
Extra long or extra large legs 25c extra. Delivered free east of Mississippi. If west, add 25c.

O MAINE TROUTING BOOT GUARANTEE
We guarantee these boots to outwear two pairs of ordinary rubber boots and will give a new pair to any dissatisfied customer. If the rubber breaks return them together with this Guarantee tag and we will replace them free of charge.
L. L. Bean
Freeport, Maine

Ration Book Case

Outside made of slate gray, heavy double texture duck, inner ration book compartments of white stiff duck. ges bound with black leather.
Size: When folded, 4¾" wide, 7" deep.
Price: 55¢ postpaid.

Notice
Due to shortage of material we are obliged to omit pages 7, 8, 9, 10. Also, 63, 64, 65 and 66.

Ladies' Bandanna Shirt

Bold bandanna print patterns on soft and comfortable all cotton fabric. Washable.
High neckband collar with long points. Long sleeves with two-button cuffs. "Tuck-in" tails may be worn in or out.
Two patterns: Navy and White. Red and White.
Ladies' sizes 8 to 16.
Price, $11.50 postpaid.

Bean's Flannel Sheets

Take the chill out of getting into bed on a cold winter's evening. Made in Canada of tightly woven and softly napped cotton with polyester whipstitched ends for strength and stability. Exceptionally cozy and comfortable, these flannel sheets are also long wearing even after many washings.

For home, camp or cottage. The sheets double as lightweight summer blankets. Machine washable and dryable, they are cut oversize to allow for normal 8% to 10% shrinkage. Cut sizes are given below. The same sized sheets can be used for top or bottom.

Three colors: White with Blue stripes. White with Pink Stripes. White with Gold stripes. (Queen size available in solid White only.)

7481N Twin Size Sheet (70"x100"), $9.00 ppd.
7488N Double Size Sheet (80"x100"), $10.00 ppd.
7489N Queen Size Sheet (90"x104"), $11.50 ppd.

TOP RATED ★★★★★
Bean's Wicked Good® Slippers

C-E. Here in Maine, "wicked good" is as good as you can get. When you slip into these soft shearling slippers, you'll understand exactly how they earned their name. Unlike similar-looking imitations, our slippers are made of superior sheepskin. Known as one of nature's best insulators, shearling draws away moisture so your feet stay warmer on chilly winter mornings. Best of all, the shearling wraps completely around your foot so you feel nothing but soft, warm fleece against your skin. All styles except Slipper have indoor/ outdoor sole. Imported. **Colors** Slippers and Scuff: Brown. Chocolate Brown. Moccasins: Brown. Chocolate Brown. Vintage Red. Natural. Classic Green. Fuchsia. Cobalt Stone.

Whole sizes Medium B 5 to 11. Half sizes order *up*.
C. SLIPPER HH105120 $59   D. MOCCASIN HH130484 $59   E. SCUFF HH272329 $59

Vintage Red   Natural   Classic Green   Fuchsia   Cobalt Stone

---

Our telephone number is Freeport UNiversity 5-6311. For rush delivery all telephone and telegraph orders must be shipped C.O.D.

Bean's Striped Flashlight

This is a very practical 2-cell flashlight. It is 7¼" long, and weighs 10 oz.

Will give the same light as any 2-cell flashlight. If dropped or laid the bright color makes it easy to find.

Price, with 2 batteries, $1.10 postpaid.

$15.25 Postpaid

New Maine Hunting Coat

So many shooting accidents occur in the big game country that everyone should take some precaution. Our new Maine Hunting Coat is so colored that it not only gives you this protection but does not frighten big game. It is a new exclusive pattern that we have been perfecting for a long time and is without doubt the best color for big game hunting of any coat we ever offered.

It has nine pockets arranged so that each article needed can be carried in a separate pocket thus avoiding rattling or breaking.

Color: green and black with yellow overplaid.

The most convenient pocket is directly in the back with opening on right outside seam. This pocket is very large and is intended for carrying lunch, game or anything bulky. Send for free sample of this new coat as we feel sure you will want one when you see the cloth. Free with every coat, blood-proof Slicker Bag as shown on page 25.

Price $15.25; with red lined reversible belt, $16.25.

NEW #31 STOCKING   **85c Postpaid**

An extra good value. Made of fine imported wool that looks and feels like camel's hair.
Color: camel brown with 2" top of red or green, a protection against accidental shooting. Length 21". Factory knit. Price 85c postpaid.

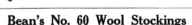

28

Bean's New Fish Bag

Is made of heavy brown duck with reinforced bottom and adjustable shoulder strap. Has two large pockets in back for carrying hooks, leaders, etc. One side is made of heavy mesh material that keeps fish much better than willow basket, as it allows free circulation of air. Closes at top with two strong snap fasteners as shown.

We believe this bag to be an improvement over willow baskets as it is less bulky and is easily cleaned.

Size 10" square by 3¾" deep.

Price $1.75 postpaid.

Leader Envelope

Is made of transparent waterproof silk. Put a very little water in envelope with leader and it will always be ready for instant use.

By putting one leader in an envelope they will not get snarled and you see at a glance the one you want.

Price 10¢; 3 for 25¢ postpaid.

Bean's June Bug Spinner

Has proved very effective for trout and all pan fish. Designed for use in streams and ponds where a free spinning spoon is necessary.

They come in hammered silver, hammered brass and hammered bronze. Size 1" x ½".

Price, all three in transparent container as shown 40¢.

Bean's No. 60 Wool Stockings

Fine soft worsted stockings made especially for us in the same design of a famous English number. Light weight, full ribbed, especially for tennis, golf, general outing and street wear.

Sizes 9½ to 13. Colors: Blue, Brown and Oxford.

Price 80¢ postpaid.

L. L. BEAN INC. FREEPORT MAINE
(Spring 1943)

functional, no-nonsense clothing and equipment that he guaranteed satisfaction. Never condescending and always mindful of his customers' bottom line ("Throwing away a pair of used 16" leather top rubbers is about the same as throwing away a $5.00 bill. Send them to us and we will make them good as new," he advised), L.L. came across as upright, upbeat, and "woods wise." He may have been hawking boots and boats, but to a country pining for escape from grim economic reality, the merchant from Freeport was also dispensing good old American optimism.

The friendly informality of the write-ups in the L.L.Bean catalog made L.L. seem an approachable adviser on all things outdoors, sort of an everyman's Maine Guide. "Everyone is welcome to call for advice on where to hunt or fish," he invited in autumn 1934. Call they did. The phone at the Freeport offices of L.L.Bean rang off the hook. In her memoir of forty-five years of service at the company, *Spillin' the Beans: Behind the Scenes at L.L.Bean*, Carlene Griffin recounted that "[L.L.] could not have imagined how many of the callers wouldn't hang up until they had reached L.L. himself. People from places as far apart as Hudson Bay and Brazil, California and India, would telephone him for advice, asking how to outfit a hunting or fishing party, or requesting information on the best

game areas for a coming trip to Maine."

Still other customers made a point of stopping in at Bean's retail store to buttonhole L.L. for his expertise. For the hunter or camper bound for the wilds of Maine, Bean was a convenient stopover. U.S. Route 1, newly resurfaced in concrete, provided the only viable access to Maine's lakes, rivers, and coastline in the days before the interstate, and the highway went right past the front door. Tourists visited Freeport in such large numbers that the village began experiencing something more familiar in big cities: traffic jams. How much of that was a result of Maine's recently minted "Vacationland" tourism-promotion campaign and how much was caused by pilgrims to L.L.Bean is hard to say. In 1937 Freeport installed its first traffic light at Main and Bow streets, right by the entrance to the retail store.

Finding L.L.'s office in the chaotic maze of rooms in the Warren Block factory was no easy task. "There wasn't any good way to get into the Bean plant," recalled L.L.'s friend, writer John Gould. "The building hadn't been built for [L.L.], and he had grown into it deviously. The outside stairway went up three floors from the sidewalk, and having mounted it you would arrive all a-pant in a little room that smelled of oil-tanned leather and rubber cement. If you persisted,

Below left: 1937 license plate. Below right: A vintage postcard depicts a Maine back road. Opposite, top: An out-of-state family stops at a Maine Publicity Bureau booth in Maine. Opposite, bottom: Beachgoers, York, Maine, undated.

"The scarlet is a good fishing shirt as red repels black flies. Also safe for dragging in deer without coat."
—L.L. Bean catalog, 1960

$2.85 Postpaid

Displaces bulky bags and suit cases

Newfangled "hookless fastener," aka zipper, used on Sportsman's Kit Bag

Purchase of Mt. Katahdin gives Baxter State Park a start

New Crawl-In Tent features "snake-proof door rise"

Hitler becomes chancellor of Germany

FDR gives America a New Deal

Average U.S. income: $1,368

Check's in the mail: Social Security enacted

1931

1934

1936

1930

1933

1935

Dust Bowl exodus exceeds two million

Maine rolls out "Vacationland" campaign

Bean incorporates, and all stock is held by family but for ten shares held by three employees

A new addition doubles L.L.Bean factory size

Future Bean president Leon Gorman born

Haul of Fame: Pack Basket makes its first appearance

62

SKIING
in the East

THE BEST TRAILS *and* HOW TO GET THERE

A GUIDE FOR WINTER SPORT FANS

$1.50

Describing over 1000 TRAILS in 216 LOCALITIES

MAINE, NEW HAMPSHIRE VERMONT, MASSACHUSETTS CONNECTICUT, NEW YORK NEW JERSEY, PENNSYLVANIA

AMERICAN GUIDE SERIES

WPA FEDERAL WRITERS' PROJECT 110 KING STREET • NEW YORK CITY

1

What Depression? Bean sales top $1 million

Freeport's first traffic light installed, right in front of retail store

Ernest Hemingway, a Bean Boot wearer, reports on Spanish Civil War

Japan invades China

First air-conditioned auto hits the road

Germany invades Poland

L.L.'s wife, Bertha, dies at age seventy-three

New item: Duck Decoys with swivel heads

Japan attacks Pearl Harbor

1938

1940

1937

1939

1941

Bean jean: Sport Dungaree unveiled

L.L. marries his post-surgical nurse, Claire Lucille Boudreau

Business Man Shirt debuts ($1.95), to be worn "going and coming from hunting grounds"

ean's "Business Man" Shirt

We have examined about every semi-d shirt manufactured east of the Mississippi F with the idea of giving our customers somet out of the ordinary to wear going and co on their outing trips.

No factory shirt in the country is made b than ours, regardless of price.

The collar has a "custom stay" which tively prevents corners from turning up. feature is found only in very high priced sl

The 3 hole pearl buttons are the stror money will buy. They won't pull off.

Shirt No. 1 is a high count broadcloth sharp blue stripe on white ground. A typical pattern worn by men who realize that simpl of pattern is the smartest shirt to wear

2   **3**

63

you'd startle various employees hidden away in random cubicles pursuing some manufacturing task. Whoever it was, he'd look up surprised that you had found him, as if only the initiated could gain admittance. He would gladly direct you to Mr. Bean's office, usually through the mailing room, stitching department, and fly-tying department. You would perhaps arrive to find a spirited discussion going on between Mr. Bean and assorted Freeporters, as to the relative merits of the .30-30 and the .32 special. All such conferences were pitched above the whir of the stitching machines."

Among the visitors who journeyed to Freeport and ascended the steep, creaky stairs to the Bean "showroom" above the post office, one in particular stood out. "Eleanor Roosevelt was in town, and word had gone out that she was to visit the store," recounted Carlene Griffin. "It was about the time of day when L.L. usually went home, but he was excited about meeting Mrs. Roosevelt, so he stayed in his office. He didn't want Mrs. Roosevelt to think he'd been waiting for her, so when he heard footsteps coming up the stairs, he picked up the phone and pretended to be talking business. His phone, however, was one of the new ones at the time and he wasn't used to it. It had a French receiver and he had put the wrong end to his ear. Apparently he realized it as his illustrious visitor came through the door and, according to our witness, he was 'all shook up.' Anyway he greeted Mrs. Roosevelt.

"Only it wasn't Mrs. Roosevelt. It was Mrs.

Clockwise from top right: Shipping room, 1936 (left to right: Ken Stilkey, Dick Marston, Phil Marston, Jim Cushing, Ermon Sawyer, Henry Allen, Wid Griffin, and Gene Reneau); L.L. in his retail-store office with his three grandsons, 1941; Oxnard and Warren Block, Freeport, mid-1930s; office area on December 8, 1931; Fly-Tying Department, 1939 (left to right: Audrey Williams, Francis Lee Stearns, Gail Stowell Griffin, and George Soule); shipping room, 1935 (Jules Soule, left, and Jim Cushing).

Winslow, the cleaning lady," continued Griffin. "For a few startled moments, she was greeted like royalty. L.L. didn't have a clue as to what Mrs. Roosevelt looked like, of course, and Mrs. Winslow had all she could do to get a word in edgewise and identify herself."

L.L. did meet the real Mrs. Roosevelt that day, and on several later occasions when the First Lady traveled overland to the family's retreat at Campobello Island on the Canadian border. (FDR himself steamed ahead in the presidential yacht, *Potomac*.) Mrs. Roosevelt proved a tough sell on that first visit, resisting the impulse to purchase fishing boots for her husband despite L.L.'s enthusiastic assistance. But L.L. wouldn't let her leave empty-handed. Ever the salesman, he presented Mrs. Roosevelt a trout knife (retail price seventy-five cents) to pass along to the president. Weeks later a letter arrived typed on White House stationery. "My dear Mr. Bean: I am very grateful to have the knife which I shall keep on my desk.

L.L. sent a trout knife—like one of those above—as a gift to the new U.S. president in 1933.

It was very kind of you to send it to me." It was signed "Franklin D. Roosevelt."

....

Visitors to the L.L.Bean factory didn't always arrive during normal business hours. Hunters and fishermen from out of state had a habit of setting off for Maine as soon as their workday concluded in Boston, New York, and points south. That often put them in Freeport during the middle of the night. Not one to let a sale slip by, L.L. installed a night bell with a card that read, "Push once a minute until clerk appears." That clerk was L.L.'s brother Henry, who, according to Gould, "looked and acted so much like L.L. that hundreds of customers thought L.L. himself stayed on duty all night."

As middle-of-the-night sales picked up, L.L.

THE WHITE HOUSE
WASHINGTON

August 5, 1933

My dear Mr. Bean:

I am very grateful to have the knife which I shall keep on my desk. It was very kind of you to send it to me.

I hope that next year if I stop in South West Harbor on my cruise, I shall have the pleasure of seeing you.

Very sincerely yours

Franklin D Roosevelt

Mr. L. L. Bean
Freeport, Maine

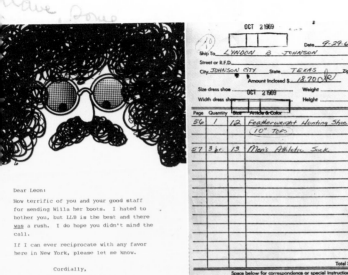

Dear Leon:

How terrific of you and your good staff for sending Willa her boots. I hated to bother you, but LLB is the best and there was a rush. I do hope you didn't mind the call.

If I can ever reciprocate with any favor here in New York, please let me know.

Cordially,

Gene Shalit.

3 March 77

OCT 2 1969

Date 9-29-69

Ship To LYNDON B JOHNSON

Street or R.F.D.

City JOHNSON CITY State TEXAS Zip

Amount Inclosed $ 18.70

Size dress shoe   Weight   Chest

Width dress shoe   OCT 2 1969   Height   Waist

Page	Quantity	Size	Article & Color		Price	
56	1	12	Featherweight Hunting Shoe (10" Tops)		16	00
57	3 pr.	13	Men's Athletic Sock		2	70
				Total $	18	70

Space below for correspondence or special instructions

Fall 1969 Catalogue

From Jay Miller Box 2748 Amarillo, Texas 79105

TED WILLIAMS, Presid
SAMMY SNEAD, Vice-Pr
ALBERT NEFF, Vice-Pr
T. WALTER KILLILEA,

Ted Williams, Inc.

P. O. BOX 48-786 - INTERNATIONAL AIRPORT - MIAMI 48, Fl

PHONE: NE5-6484
CABLE: TEDWIL

November 9, 1960

Mr. L. L. Bean
Freeport, Maine

Dear Mr. Bean:

As you know my career as an active ball player is over and it is now my intention to devote more time to my fishing tackle business.

With this in mind, we are planning to expand our operations to include other sportsmen's items.

As I have visited your plant and used your products I am familiar, in a way, with your company, hence the reason for this letter.

I would appreciate your advising me if you would be interested in merging with Ted Williams, Inc. or, if not, would you consider the outright sale of your company and if so, on what terms.

If either of the above propositions interests you kindly advise me at your earliest convenience.

I ♥ BEAN

Few companies can claim customers as fiercely loyal, legion, and diverse as those of L.L.Bean. Devotees of the brand return again and again—often over several decades—for the products they've come to know and love. So it's hardly a surprise to learn that Bean counts among its admirers luminaries such as movie stars, politicians, and American sports heroes. Presidents Lyndon Johnson and Dwight Eisenhower considered themselves fans, baseball legend Babe Ruth donned Bean Boots when on the hunting trail, and Ted Williams felt such passion for the company he tried to outright buy the whole thing. Bean boasts plenty of present-day enthusiasts as well: alongside paparazzi photos of current celebrities in Prada and Jimmy Choos, you'll also see the rich and famous sporting iconic Bean products ranging from boots to bags and beyond.

Above, from left: A letter from Gene Shalit thanking Leon Gorman for rushing him a pair of Bean boots; Lyndon Johnson's order form for the Featherweight Hunting Shoe; an offer from Ted Wiliams to buy the company. Opposite, clockwise from top left: Julia Roberts with a Boat and Tote; Rachel McAdams and Babe Ruth in Bean Boots; President Bill Clinton visits the flagship store in Freeport; Tom Brokaw in a Bean jacket; President George W. Bush is gifted a pair of Bean Boots; Smoky Joe Wood in Bean Boots.

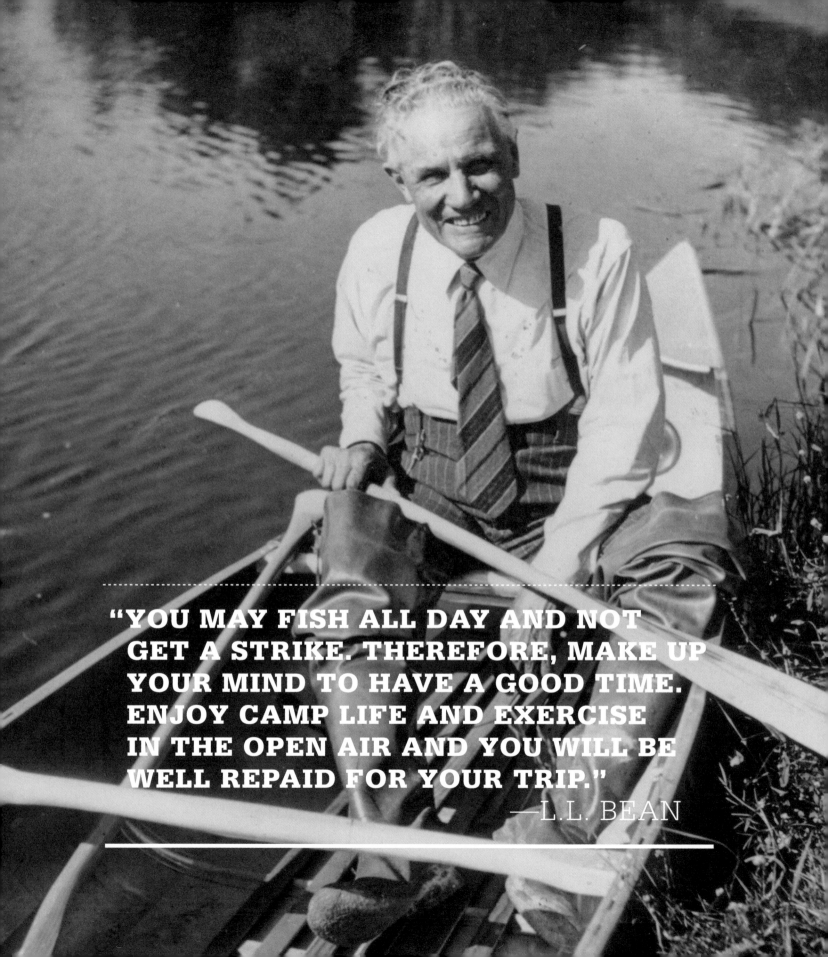

"YOU MAY FISH ALL DAY AND NOT GET A STRIKE. THEREFORE, MAKE UP YOUR MIND TO HAVE A GOOD TIME. ENJOY CAMP LIFE AND EXERCISE IN THE OPEN AIR AND YOU WILL BE WELL REPAID FOR YOUR TRIP."

—L.L. BEAN

came up with an off-the-wall idea: why not stay open around the clock? Twenty-four-hour service, which would become a hallmark of L.L.Bean and help secure the company's mythical standing in the hearts of several generations of New Englanders, might have seemed outlandish for a small company located deep in Maine. And it might also have violated Maine's "blue laws" restricting store hours during the week and prohibiting opening on Sundays. But for L.L. it was an extension of his philosophy that the customer always came first. After a one-year trial staying open all night, L.L. reduced store hours to twenty hours. He would later revisit twenty-four-hour retailing, effectively throwing away the key to his showroom, but not until 1951.

L.L. had one more daring leap in him as the Depression decade came to a close. He got to work writing a book to share the accumulated know-how of his nearly fifty years of pursuing big game, waterfowl, and fish throughout Maine. For a man of meager schooling, this was no small undertaking. But in the interest of efficiency around the office and to gain some measure of peace from the parade of callers seeking his words of wisdom, L.L. had to do something. The result, *Hunting, Fishing, and Camping*, published in 1942, was all business. "The object of this book is not to bore my readers with personal yarns and experiences but to give definite information in the fewest words possible….The instructions are so condensed that the reading time of the whole book is only 85 minutes," wrote L.L. in the introduction.

Opposite: A photo from a 1941 *Life* magazine article. Top: L.L. shoots skeet at 1939 picnic. Above: A spring 1938 catalog page. Left: L.L.'s homemade fish silhouette commemorated a large catch.

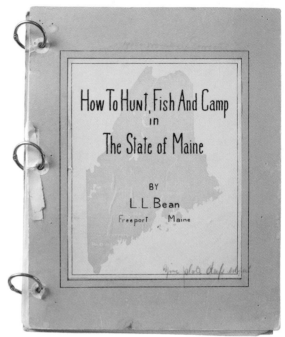

Above left: A hooded Mallard Coat from the 1920s showcases a popular Bean duck pattern. Above right: A corrected manuscript for an early version of *Hunting, Fishing, and Camping*. Opposite: Spring 1939 catalog cover.

As well as laying out advice on how to hunt black bear and build a bough bed, the book presented L.L.'s outdoor credo. "I am a firm believer in the conservation of all fish and game and the strict enforcement of all game laws," he stated. "To my mind hunting and fishing is the big lure that takes us into the great open spaces and teaches us to forget the mean and petty things of life."

Getting his book into print took some doing. "I happen to know that one big publisher had a chance at Bean's book—but there were split infinitives, and the prose was jerky, and it didn't sound like much," recalled Gould. "Bean decided publishers didn't know everything, so he put the book together, printed it on his own presses, and sold it from his own catalog." L.L. soon had a runaway best seller on his hands, selling more than 150,000 copies at a dollar apiece. To this day, participants in L.L.Bean Outdoor Discovery school overnights find a copy of *Hunting, Fishing, and Camping* resting on the bedside table inside their tent cabin. As part of its one-hundredth-anniversary celebration in 2012, Bean is rereleasing *Hunting, Fishing, and Camping*, including a special introduction and annotations by L.L.'s great grandson, Bill Gorman.

CHAPTER 3

THE WAR YEARS

The **FIELD COAT**	First sold in **1947**

THE SECOND WORLD WAR BROUGHT AMERICA TOGETHER AND BROUGHT L.L.BEAN TO WASHINGTON, AS IT OUTFITTED SERVICEMEN WITH BOOTS AND OUTERWEAR. BACK IN MAINE, L.L. CONTINUED TO BUILD A BOOMING BUSINESS THAT WAS BECOMING A HOUSEHOLD NAME THANKS TO SAVVY MERCHANDISING, GREAT PRESS, AND HIS GOLDEN RULE: "SELL GOOD MERCHANDISE AT A REASONABLE PROFIT, TREAT YOUR CUSTOMERS LIKE HUMAN BEINGS, AND THEY WILL ALWAYS COME BACK FOR MORE."

orm didn't follow function in the execution of the Field Coat so much as it stayed on the sidelines, out of harm's way. The coat was designed with one thing in mind: shooting easily spooked, explosively fast ducks, as well as quail, grouse, pheasant, and other upland game birds.

The coat's bi-swing back—an extra panel of fabric pleated at the shoulder—and gusseted underarms gave a hunter full range of motion. Five pockets warmed hands and held gloves, hat, sandwich, and other necessities for a full day of hunting. Extra-tough, high-grade cotton duck fabric sloughed off brambles and briars. And, finally, that distinctive "brush brown" color, hued like meadow grass hit by a hard freeze, helped a hunter to blend in during autumn hunting season.

The Field Coat was an instant favorite following its introduction to the Bean catalog in 1924. Back then it was called the Maine Duck Hunting Coat, before L.L. renamed it the Field Coat in 1947. Hunters, naturally, were its primary customer, drawn by the coat's utilitarian design and such thoughtful details as loops for shotgun shells inside the front pockets, another loop at the nape of the collar for displaying a hunting license, and a rubber-lined pocket called a "game bag" on the inside of the coat in the lumbar region. "The game bag had a flap mounted vertically. The idea was you'd open the flap, stick your dead birds in there, and keep going," says A.J. Curran, Bean's director of product for outerwear and accessories. Hunters quickly discovered another benefit of the game bag, as Tom Mahoney and Leonard Sloane explained in

Maine Duck Hunting Coat

$7.75

Is made of highest grade olive green duck with soft Corduroy faced collar and cuffs. The texture is very tight and water-proofed.

Briars and underbrush will not snag this material. Neither friction or long service effects its water-proof quality. It is the toughest fabric known.

Both inside and outside is made of same material, including pockets and top sleeve.

Four outside lower pockets protected by flaps, con-

Left: 1924 catalog advertisement. Opposite: L.L. wears the Maine Duck Hunting Coat for a 1941 *Life* magazine photo shoot.

With the whole of the country engaged in the war effort—either fighting abroad or working at home—leisure time, frivolity, and raw materials were scarce. L.L. did his part by using his Down East know-how to make better boots on the ground (and the decks) for the armed services. Meanwhile, despite leaner budgets, Bean's original customers, hunters, provided a steady demand for the rugged, practical, and durable gear they knew they could count on.

Bean's Pack Basket

Vessel? Work of art? Hamper? Woven by hand from seasoned white ash, the Pack Basket is made by a tribe of Maine Native Americans that has earned its living for the last century by making baskets. The 1941 catalog described its capacity as "4 pecks."

New Maine Hunting Coat

The virtually waterproof wool coat comes in a handsome plaid and even has matching pants. Still, it's rugged enough for serious outdoorsmen. (Back in the day, it could be ordered with a Blood-proof Game Bag.)

Boots

Bean Boots like this vintage pair from during WWII featured black synthetic soles due to rubber rationing.

L.L.Bean Staff Model: Kurt Heisler

Years at Bean: 6
Hobbies: Hunting, especially bow hunting, with traditional equipment (1960s and 1970s recurve bows and homemade cedar arrows); camping; canoeing; hiking; backpacking; and cross-country skiing.
Accomplishments: A 2010 "Bean's Best" recipient and an award-winning designer of L.L.Bean products such as the Bigelow Pack, Waterproof Sling Pack, Waxed Cotton Pack Basket, and Fish Chest Pack, as well as the (non-L.L.Bean) Extreme Cold Weather Tent for the U.S. Special Forces, the Marine Combat Tent (used in the Gulf War), and the tents used on Eric Simonson's 1999 and 2001 Everest expeditions.
Passions: "I love the outdoors, but my passion is making gear that gets *other* people outdoors."
Favorite Bean Product: "The Maine Hunting Shoe. I have at least four pairs."

a profile of L.L. Bean in their 1966 classic *The Great Merchants*. "Bean's Field Coat, with a game pocket that lets down to serve as a waterproof seat, is another product of L.L.'s fertile brain—described by gunners who previously had to sit on a frosty log as one of the greatest inventions since the wheel," they wrote.

It's doubtful the Field Coat would still be in production if it were all about function with no flair. L.L. clearly had an eye for fashion when he introduced the coat to the catalog, as he did with other such classic apparel items. The Field Coat's length, its drape (some might call it a comfortable slouch), and the rakish look of the contrasting dark olive green, fine-wale corduroy trim on the collar, and inside cuffs speak to a well-honed design sensibility that also appealed to nonhunters. "That style of coat was used by ranch hands and hunters well before L.L. got a hold of it," says Curran. "But by making it look different from any other coat out there, he made it an iconic piece."

During the postwar years, the Field Coat began showing up on college and prep-school campuses in the Northeast, then exploded in popularity during the preppy boom of the late 1970s and early 1980s. Washed repeatedly to achieve that all-important scruff, the Field Coat may have been, at least initially, "the epitome of anti-fashion," as the *Fashion Encyclopedia* declared of all L.L.'s early garments, but it had earned a rugged cachet.

It was in the mid-1990s that L.L.Bean decided to reconcile the Field Coat's split personality by spinning off a casual lifestyle version of the coat. Designers "detuned" the coat, in Curran's words, by stripping out hunter-specific elements like the game bag, shell loops, and hunting-license loop. (All of those features are still found on the waxed canvas Upland Field Coat sold in the Hunting

Above: L.L. Bean and his brother Guy Bean with Levi Patterson, all of Freeport, Maine, after a hunting trip to Dew Drop Inn, 1944.

1-4-03

To L.L. Bean
From: Shirley A. Stearns

My children:
  Chris, Suprina, Miles Schmidt
  David, Connie, Tate Schmidt
  Jeriny, Larry, Nicole Ziglar
  Joe, Julie, Evelyn Schmidt
  Tom Schmidt.

Enclosed are pictures of my children wearing their Adirondack Barn Jackets and Ear warmers my gift to them for Christmas (I also have a jacket & ear warmer but didn't get into the picture)

when I ordered them in Nov. one of the clerks said there was a contest last year and for me to send pictures. Since then I understand that the contest was only for the LL Bean 90th Anniversity but they told me to send pictures anyway.

I want to thank everyone I talked to at LL Bean for their patience and cooperation when I sort of became confused with the size and colors. All turned out ok. What a happy time I had surprising them and they were surprised

Thank You Again
Shirley Stearns

100 YEARS OF STAYING WARM

IN MAINE, THEY KNOW COLD. BEAN COATS HAVE BEEN WARDING OFF THE COLD
SINCE THE FIELD COAT'S DEBUT.

"There has been a lot of snow this winter and our very active two-year-old insisted on helping with the shoveling despite freezing temperatures and wind. Wrapped up in his L.L.Bean jacket, boots, and snow pants, he stayed warm and even came back in with dry feet! Thanks to L.L.Bean, my driveway gets shoveled and I get 45 minutes of peace and quiet while our son is outside with his dad!"

—Amanda Harris, Tolland, Connecticut,
March 22, 2011

"I am a volunteer nature docent wearing a model 1972 Field Coat accompanied by a six-inch-long banana slug (*Ariolimax californicus*). In the past 17 years, I have worn the jacket on about 300 two-hour nature hikes for schoolkids. This coat has served me well on the trails, and in September it started all over again—not the slug, he's retired."

—Forrest S., Belmont, CA

"A compliment on your women's Penobscot Parka that I purchased probably late '70s or early '80s—and still have! It is a very warm coat. You did well. It was 9 degrees this morning with a good wind and I was quite comfortable in it."

—Ann Young, Santa Fe,
New Mexico, January 5, 2004

"I am having trouble with my goose down hooded pullover with coyote fur trim. Namely, my fourteen-year-old granddaughter Maggie has taken a liking to it. You sent it to me in 1961. During the '70s, '80s, and '90s we did a lot of backpacking in the mountains of eastern Tennessee and western North Carolina. One of us always had it stuffed in our backpack during winter hikes. Our son and daughter got a lot of use out of it during their teenage years. As you can see, it's not showing much sign of wear yet, but even L.L. stuff can't last forever. So, if you have any more stashed away somewhere, please send four more. Any size will do."

—John McLeod, Valdosta, Georgia,
August 5, 2006

WOW

WAAC

WAVE

ARMY NURSE

NAVY NURSE

RED CROSS

She's a **WOW**
WOMAN ORDNANCE WORKER

Adolph Treidler's 1942 poster encouraged women to fill in on the factory floor while men were fighting overseas.

catalog.) They tinkered with the canvas used in the shell, retaining the same heft and durability but giving it a more textured weave as well as a relaxed, worn-in look right off the rack.

At Bean, heritage garments like the Field Coat present an interesting balancing act for product managers like Curran, who want to retain the item's traditional appeal while updating it as better processes or materials become available, or as trends and lifestyles change. The Field Coat's canvas shell has recently been given a special treatment that makes it more water-resistant, its bi-swing shoulders were overhauled to work better, and the interior seam edges are now finished with nylon edge tape to reduce binding. Yet the coat still comes as always with three buttons made of tagua nut, a natural material with unrivaled hardness, harvested from the Central and South American rain forest. Sure, plastic buttons would be cheaper and nearly as good, but why mess with a good thing? "If we make a change, we make it purposeful and thoughtful," says Curran. "The Field Coat remains aesthetically true to L.L.'s original."

....

After the Japanese attacked Pearl Harbor on December 7, 1941, and Franklin D. Roosevelt declared war against Germany four days later, America rolled up its sleeves on the home front and got to work supporting an all-out war on two stages. Unemployment lines and work camps were quickly replaced by belching steel mills and assembly plants clamoring for workers to stoke round-the-clock production. With millions of draft-age men called into military service, women filled the gap by heading to the factory floor in unprecedented numbers. Wages improved, but there wasn't much to buy, as basic goods like

NORTHWOODS AMBASSADORS

LEGENDARY FOR THEIR WOODS WISDOM, MAINE GUIDES ARE AN EXCLUSIVE BUNCH, AND THEY'RE EMPLOYED THROUGHOUT L.L.BEAN.

Wild Maine is no place for beginners. Its nine- to twelve-foot ocean tides are devilish, its rivers big and powerful, and its woods dark and tangled. Whether you're hunting, fishing, or boating, it helps to have a knowledgeable escort. That's been the calling of Maine Guides since they were legislated into existence in 1897.

In a state that prides itself on outdoor heritage, the roughly four thousand Maine Guides are a big deal. The first registered Maine Guide was Cornilia "Fly Rod" Crosby, who once landed two hundred trout in one day and slew Maine's last legal caribou. She caused a sensation by wearing a knee-length doeskin skirt at the first annual Sportsmen's Show at New York's Madison Square Garden.

"It definitely became cool to be a Maine Guide in the late 1980s and '90s, with a boomlet in the number of guides," says Don Kleiner, executive director of the Maine Professional Guide Association.

Anyone guiding paying clients into the outdoors in Maine has to be registered with the state's Department of Inland Fisheries and Wildlife. And the only way to register is by passing a rigorous part-written, part-oral exam in one of five specialized areas—hunting, fishing, recreation, sea kayaking, or tidewater fishing.

Peter Bergh is a sea kayak guide with Bean's Outdoor Discovery School (ODS) and a registered Maine Guide. "Being a Maine Guide gives you fundamental skills in group management, first aid, weather, navigation, and camping that set the baseline at a high level," he says. "Then at Bean, all of the instructors work to raise the

bar higher through a lot of training and note sharing." The Outdoor Discovery School even offers a Registered Maine Sea Kayak Guide Course ($499) that prepares enrollees for the state exam.

About fifty registered Maine Guides work for the ODS as active guides. Another one hundred or so work throughout the company in a variety of non-guide jobs. Mike Gawtry is director of sporting equipment and a registered Maine Guide. "In product development, we are constantly trying to identify the 'next great idea' that solves a problem for our customers," he says. "When guiding, it is essentially the same objective: trying to find the next idea that makes for a superior experience for the client.

"A perfect example is a product like canoe seats," Gawtry continues. "I know from experience that if I can help keep a person comfortable while sitting for long periods of time in a canoe, I have a better chance of getting them to fish. By developing or supplying a canoe seat that provides the best lower-back support and cushion, I can help a person stay out three to four more hours, getting them into the evening hours when some of the best hatches occur."

When you hire a registered Maine Guide, you can be confident of retaining someone who is competent, reliable and woods wise, says Kleiner. If lucky, you might not have cause to appreciate their real value. "Anyone can guide when things are going well. It's when things go bad that a guide is put to the test," says Kleiner. "With a Maine Guide, you can be completely confident you will have a good time and return safely."

From top: Maine Guides and L.L.Bean employees Mike Gawtry and Peter Bergh.

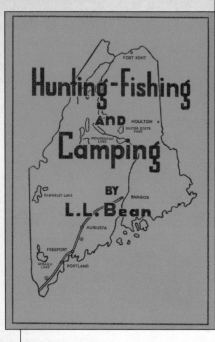

by far the best
stove we ever
d. Made of brass
steel legs, as
n. Made espe-
for kerosene, the
of all fuel oils.

throws out a
like a blow
nutes. Ask a GI

age only 8½" x

D-day opens second front against Hitler

Doris Day has hit with "Sentimental Journey"

G.I. Bill of Rights enacted

THE BEAN CENTURY

How-to guru: L.L. publishes _Hunting, Fishing, and Camping_

Mr. Bean goes to Washington, advises Pentagon on cold-weather apparel and other gear

U.S. defeats Japanese fleet at Midway

1943

1945

1942

1944

Bean accepts War Savings Stamps as payment

Same as cash: the new Ration Book Carrier

New Cool-Ray Sun Glasses meet U.S. Army Air Corps specs

Allies retake Sicily

FDR dies

V-E day on May 8

Bean begins issuing cash bonus to employees, approaching 25 percent in good years

First computer, ENIAC, weighs thirty tons

Atomic bomb hits Hiroshima

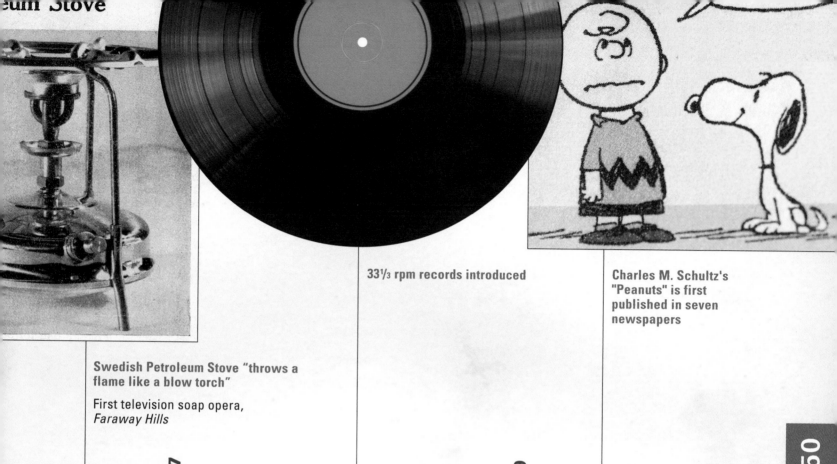

33⅓ rpm records introduced

Charles M. Schultz's
"Peanuts" is first
published in seven
newspapers

Swedish Petroleum Stove "throws a
flame like a blow torch"

First television soap opera,
Faraway Hills

1947

1949

1946

1948

1950

Chain-tread sole added to the Maine
Hunting Shoe

Start of Cold War

Hear me now? Cell phone invented

Volkswagon Beetle comes
to America

In reply refer to
SPQRD 201
Bean, L. L.

Army Service Forces
Office of the Quartermaster General
Washington 25, D. C.

19 December 1945

Mr. L. L. Bean
President, L. L. Bean Company
Freeport, Maine

Dear Mr. Bean:

This office wishes to express its appreciation and commendation to you and the personnel of your company for the loyalty, unceasing effort, and many contributions afforded the Quartermaster Corps during the past few years.

Your excellent work and technical assistance in connection with such important items for the soldier as winter footgear, more specifically Shoe Pacs, are fully recognized and greatly appreciated by the entire Quartermaster Corps. No one realizes more than this office the importance of the time, effort, and skill which have been so fully devoted by your company in helping this office to improve this item for use by troops in the field.

I personally want you to know that your many contributions will long be remembered and recognized by the Quartermaster Corps as playing a vital part in the total effort to help bring victory to our Country. It is hoped that you will continue to be interested in our post-war program of improving existing Quartermaster items and in the development of new ones.

Very truly yours,

GEORGES F. DORIOT
Brigadier General, QMC
Director, Military Planning Division

C O P Y

gasoline, paper, sugar, coffee, shoes, and anything made of rubber or steel were rationed in the name of steering raw materials into war production.

Still bruised from the dislocations and hardships of the Great Depression, America was being wrenched again by seismic social and economic shifts. As grim news poured in from overseas, few had the time or energy for seemingly frivolous pursuits like camping or hunting, and L.L.Bean was in a holding pattern. New products still hit the catalog regularly, like the Red Felt Hat, Duck Call, and Bean Gym Shoe, and sewing operations in Freeport expanded into the newly built Gorman Building near the main factory, but L.L.'s attention was elsewhere. Specifically, down in Washington, D.C.

Early in the war, the War Department recruited L.L. to assist the Quartermaster Corps in devising cold-weather apparel for the Army. The special committee on which he served got hung up on one aspect of footwear. There was disagreement over the height of the rubber-bottomed, leather-topped boots under consideration. On one side were younger committee members from the West and South, who advocated for sixteen- or eighteen-inch boots. On the other side was L.L., who bristled at the extraneous use of scarce leather. "I, coming from a colder climate and having tramped through the woods for many years, knew from experience that a high boot would bind the leg muscles of a man who had to be on his feet all day, so that he would soon be lame and sore and unable to walk at all," wrote L.L. in his autobiography. "I was in favor of the 10-inch height I had used so much."

To make his case, L.L. computed that the eight ounces of surplus leather in each eighteen-inch boot would cause an infantryman to lift 4,620 unnecessary pounds during the course of a normal day's seven-mile hike. "We finally compromised and a 12-inch boot was adopted," said L.L. "The result was that later we were given

Opposite, top to bottom: A letter of thanks from the U.S. Army to L.L. Bean, December 1945; a Bean machete from the 1940s. Top: A gift suggestion from the spring 1943 catalog.
Bottom: "Letter to a P.O.W.," spring 1944 catalog.

a large order for 12-inch leather-top rubbers. These were made on the pattern of our Maine Hunting Shoe."

The navy called in 1943. Back to Washington L.L. went to advise on the production of an oceangoing version of his boot with nonslip soles suited to wet and icy decks. L.L. was particularly proud of a simple and ingenious quick-release fastening method devised by his son Carl to allow sailors washed overboard to shed their boots in a hurry. Instead of tying from the bottom up, the boot would lace from the top down, leaving a small loop the unfortunate sailor could tug to pull the laces entirely free. (Don't worry if you don't understand how that worked; only a few people alive today can figure it out.)

Once more before the war's end L.L. went off to Washington, this time to help design a canvas-and-leather map case for navigators. "We finally came to a decision on the proper size, number of compartments, etc., and were given an order to make up to 40,000 of them. Later we heard from many of the officers who had used them, and how they carried the cases all around the world after their training was completed."

It was on one such tour of duty in the nation's capital that L.L. revealed his true Mainer character, as recounted in the *Saturday Evening Post*:

During the war, a general leaving the Pentagon Building found himself sharing a taxicab to downtown Washington with a civilian. In the casual taxicab conversation that developed, the civilian named his hometown as Freeport, Maine. The general's interest brightened at once.

"Freeport?" he said. "That's L.L. Bean's town."

"Ay-yah," the man from Maine agreed. "'Tis."

"There's a man I'd sure like to meet," said

FALL 1942

Notice
Rebuilding of all types of shoes by attaching Rubber Bottoms discontinued. See Important Information on page 22C.

L.L. BEAN Inc. MANUFACTURERS FREEPORT, MAINE

Top: The fall 1942 catalog cover, with a wartime note. Bottom: L.L.Bean employees (from left to right: Ralph "Newt" Winslow, Lucille Johnson, and Russell Dyer) survey Maine Hunting Shoes being assembled for a government order.

the general. "L.L. Bean. I discovered him four or five years ago, and I've been buying from him ever since. By George, it's wonderful the way that man figures out just what you need for hunting and fishing. You hunt or fish?"

"Ay-yah," said the Freeporter, "do a lot of it. Always use Bean's things, too. Now you take Bean's duck-hunting coat—"

The conversation had hit high gear, and continued, an exchange of hunting and fishing experiences, well interlarded with tributes to the equipment and clothing sold by the mail-order house of L.L.Bean, all the way to the hotel where the civilian was getting out. As he stepped from the cab, he extended his hand.

"Pleased to meet you, General," he said. "My name's L.L. Bean."

That particular article, "The Discovery of L.L. Bean," by Arthur Bartlett in 1946, put the merchandiser from Maine on the national radar. The *Saturday Evening Post* was at the time the largest-circulation weekly magazine in the country, and the four-and-a-half-page article with color photos was overwhelmingly flattering. Bartlett labeled L.L. "a national institution and a national character," "a powerful, vigorous, dominatingly positive individual, with more than a passing resemblance to a State-of-Maine moose," and "essentially a small-town Yankee running an old-fashioned country store by mail."

On the heels of that article, inquiries and orders poured in. L.L. Bean had received a similarly glowing tribute in *Life* magazine a few years prior, but the Japanese attack on Pearl Harbor mere days following its publication had squelched any positive publicity. The *Saturday Evening Post* article paid immediate and long-lasting dividends, which L.L. happily quantified. "To have bought this space [in the magazine] would have cost us about $53,000," he wrote in his autobiography.

STATE OF BEAN

The nation may have claimed him, but Leon Leonwood Bean was Maine-born and Maine-bred. He owned camps and cottages—spare, rustic affairs—all over the state, wherever Atlantic salmon, ducks, and bear were thick. His knowledge of the best hunting and fishing grounds was encyclopedic and regularly sought by regular customers, presidents and a maharaja or two.

Haynesville was the upland home of the Dew Drop Inn.

Kingfield was home to the Pine Tree Hunting Club, which started with L.L., his brothers, Levi Patterson, Bill Libby, Arthur Gould, Ted Goldrup, and anybody who knew where L.L. had hidden the key.

L.L. Bean's childhood home from the mid-1870s until 1884 was at a farmstead in **Allenville.**

Mt. Katahdin is the tallest mountain in Maine.

L.L. built a duck-hunting camp at **Merrymeeting Bay.**

L.L. was born on a farm on Howe Hill in **Greenwood.**

Acadia National Park preserves much of Mount Desert Island.

L.L. shot his first deer in **Hastings, Maine,** while on a hunting trip with Louvie Swett.

Freeport is the home of the L.L.Bean store.

Although he now has more than 100 employees, Bean still follows the business methods of a country storekeeper. Here he helps out during a rush in the packing-and-shipping division.

The mail-order house is thoughtfully located above the post office in Freeport, Maine—a familiar address to explorers, big-game hunters and thousands of plain American sportsmen.

Each item in his catalogue is personally recommended—even fishing flies are tested.

The Discovery of L. L. Bean

By ARTHUR BARTLETT

With a passion for sports rivaled only by his passion for trade, this State-of-Mainer parlayed a pair of hunting boots into a million-dollar mail-order business . . . and also made himself a national character.

DURING the war, a general leaving the Pentagon Building found himself sharing a taxicab to downtown Washington with a civilian. In the casual taxicab conversation that developed, the civilian named his home town as Freeport, Maine. The general's interest brightened at once.

"Freeport?" he said. "That's L. L. Bean's town."

"Ay-yah," the man from Maine agreed. "'Tis."

"There's a man I'd sure like to meet," said the general. "L. L. Bean. I discovered him four or five years ago, and I've been buying from him ever since. By George, it's wonderful the way that man figures out just what you need for hunting and fishing. You hunt or fish?"

"Ay-yah," said the Freeporter, "do a lot of it. Always use Bean's things too. Now, you take Bean's duck-hunting coat ——"

The conversation had hit high gear, and continued, an exchange of hunting and fishing experiences, well interlarded with tributes to the equipment and clothing sold by the mail-order house of L. L. Bean, all the way to the hotel where the civilian was getting out. As he stepped from the cab, he extended his hand. "Pleased to meet you, general," he said. "My name's L. L. Bean."

Bean, a huge, booming-voiced State-of-Mainer, now in his early seventies, who dreamed up a new kind of hunting shoe thirty-five years ago and made it the foundation of a mail-order sporting-goods busi-

PHOTOGRAPHY BY DAVID ROBBINS

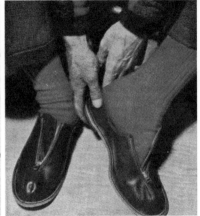

"The article brought out and developed a rather unique and unexpected angle," remembered L.L. "My father had a brother who went west years ago, and I had lost track of many of the offspring of this branch of the family. As a result of the article, these relatives, some distant and some not too far away, at about Christmas time sent cards, wrote letters and enclosed snapshots or portraits, to such an extent that I now have a more nearly complete Bean family album than would otherwise have been possible." To L.L., December 14, 1946, the publication date of Bartlett's lengthy feature story, "is one outstanding date in my business life that I will never forget."

·····························

L.L. Bean did not attend business school. He knew nothing of *The 7 Habits of Highly Successful People* or *Good to Great*. He built his company instead on intuition and common sense, doing what came naturally to him, which invariably meant doing things the right way. As a result of his success, the quirky cataloger from the far northeastern corner of the country pioneered business practices in the areas of customer service, direct marketing, order fulfillment, and brand identity that became studied and widely emulated by his direct competitors.

In the area of customer service, L.L. was far ahead of his time, and to this day, his customer-first philosophy infuses every aspect of L.L.Bean's business. The overarching principle is known at Bean as L.L.'s Golden Rule: "Sell

Opposite and above: Details from the *Saturday Evening Post* article that made L.L.Bean a household name nationwide.

THE FACE OF BEAN: ETHEL WILLIAMS

Company presidents think they're in charge, but it's their secretaries who wield real authority. That was never more true than in the case of Ethel Williams, L.L.'s secretary. As L.L. pushed into his seventies, he became less of a presence around the Freeport offices. He spent half the year in Florida, and when he was in Freeport, he was often in the office for only a few hours each morning.

Crucial decisions still flowed through L.L., which put Williams in a key gatekeeping role. That was only the beginning of her clout, something Leon Gorman (the eventual company president) quickly assessed on joining the company in the early 1960s. "It was a wonder the company functioned at all. In fact, it did because in reality it was being run by Ethel and Jessie Beal, L.L.'s son Carl's secretary. If you wanted to get something done, you worked through the two of them," he wrote in his book *L.L. Bean: The Making of an American Icon.*

"Ethel ran L.L.Bean's catalog production and advertising program," said Leon. "L.L. gave overall approval, but Ethel did all of the preparatory work and follow-up, coaxing and cajoling

L.L. and his rubber stamp into making the right decisions. Ethel dealt with the buyers, the ad agency, and the printer."

Along with Leon, Williams convinced L.L. to okay a thirty-two-page Christmas circular in 1963 that proved pivotal in company history. Bean's products were drifting toward irrelevance, and L.L.'s reluctance to alter the offerings in the spring and fall catalogs held firm. Because the circular would fly below L.L.'s radar, Williams and the young Leon Gorman took it as their one chance to modernize the company's lineup. By the time L.L. died, their efforts had retooled Bean's line of merchandise.

Williams proved invaluable in helping Leon bring coherence to the spring and fall catalogs, which had of late been ruled by whim rather than strategy. "Ethel and I built racks and paperboard page holders on which we laid out all 100-plus pages of whatever catalog we were working on…. Overall we made the catalog easier to use and, I believe, more informative," wrote Leon.

Williams started her career in 1937 and retired in 1975.

From left: Ethel Williams in 1975; Williams taking dictation from L.L. in October 1962.

good merchandise at a reasonable profit, treat your customers like human beings, and they will always come back for more."

Among the other L.L. quotes that remain touchstones for the company are:

"Above all, we wish to avoid having a dissatisfied customer";

"We consider our customers a part of our organization, and we want them to feel free to make any criticism they see fit in regard to our merchandise or service"; and

"A customer is the most important person ever in this office—in person or by mail."

L.L.'s major innovations—ironclad guarantee, 24/7 retail hours, thirty-six-hour order turn-around, and free delivery—flowed from these core beliefs. Each in its way satisfied customer need and built loyalty. "What L.L. did was take the customer's doubt out of the equation," says Curt Barry, president of F. Curtis Barry & Company, which consults the e-commerce, catalog, and retail industries on improving operations and fulfillment. "From the get-go, the DNA of the company has been to deliver what they promise.

"Before credit cards and 800 numbers, you would have sent off cash or check to place a mail order. That takes a high degree of trust. Also, you can't tell from a catalog photo how a product is made, whether it fits you right, whether you like the color," says Barry. "The Bean guarantee and postage-paid return removed any doubt.

"There are many companies today that don't get customer service right like Bean. They put limits on customer service; they're looking for the cheap way out."

Part of treating customers like human beings, to L.L.'s way of thinking, was respecting their time. He knew that when a fisherman needs waders, he wants them this weekend. But that wasn't how the mail-order business in L.L.'s time worked. "Please allow six to eight weeks for

Top: L.L.'s 1946 interview with "Big George" Hunter, which took place at George's Freeport-based grain store, was transmitted over Maine's WPOR radio station. Bottom: L.L. standing behind the counter with his brother Guy in the Fishing Department of the L.L.Bean retail store, 1948.

delivery," was the industry's standard refrain. L.L. couldn't abide that. He forever preached, "You can't sell from an empty cart." For L.L., receiving an order and getting it out the door in under thirty-six hours was a point of pride and a constant area in which the staff directed its Yankee ingenuity. The means may not have been pretty—Mahoney and Sloane in *The Great Merchants* termed the Bean factory "chaotic"— but the end was a "phenomenally successful business" in their judgment.

A distinct advantage in L.L.Bean's early success was L.L. himself—not L.L. the businessman but the outsize, amiable character the public perceived as L.L. In today's business parlance, "brand building" is all about personality. Personality breeds loyalty and sets you apart from the competition. It's why General Mills invented Betty Crocker and General Motors concocted Mr. Goodwrench. But L.L. was real, and his friendliness and knowledge came through loud and clear when the Bean catalog showed up in the mailbox twice a year. "Before anybody else thought of it, Bean really built a brand," says Jack Schmid, president of direct-marketing consultants, J. Schmid & Associates.

For L.L., making a brand of himself was an unconscious act, as Arthur Bartlett understood back in 1946 when he wrote: "It seems to be an almost universal illusion among his customers that Bean is a personal discovery, to be cherished as a rare and rich curiosity. Bean, as a shrewd businessman, does his best to foster that impression, but it doesn't take much effort. All he really has to do is be himself."

Above: Wid Griffin, left, and Maurice Hilton assemble fishing orders, March 16, 1949. Left: Shipping room, packing line, 1949 (front to back: unknown, Ada Cushing, Hazel Stetson, Virginia Davis, Mary Dyer, Pinny Allen, and Art Leavitt). Opposite: L.L. on the spring 1946 catalog cover with his wife and his son-in-law, John Gorman, during a fishing trip to Canada.

L. L. Bean, Inc.

Manufacturer
Freeport, Maine

Spring Catalog, 1946

CHAPTER 4

COLD WAR, COOL SALES

The **BOAT AND TOTE**	First sold in **1944**

THE POSTWAR YEARS SHOULD HAVE BEEN A BOOM TIME FOR L.L.BEAN. MORE THAN EVER, AMERICANS HAD TIME AND MONEY TO BURN, AND YET DURING THE '50S, SALES PLATEAUED. THE TROUBLE LAY WITH L.L., WHO IN 1960 CONTINUED TO RUN THE BUSINESS MUCH AS HE HAD FOUR DECADES EARLIER. ENTER LEON GORMAN, L.L.'S GRANDSON, A NATURALLY SAVVY MARKETER WHO REVAMPED THE CATALOG AND MODERNIZED THE ENTIRE OPERATION. BY 1967, SALES HAD DOUBLED.

Ice didn't always come tumbling out of a freezer dispenser at the push of a button. You hauled big blocks of it to a beach or lake house because there was no freezer. Your home circa 1955 had a refrigerator, but that sputtering appliance's small freezer compartment was usually so crammed with frost you were lucky to fit a single ice tray inside. Block ice lasted the better part of a vacation week if you were diligent about keeping the door to the ice chest closed. The trick was transporting it from the nearest distributor without having ice melt all over the car. Problem identified, problem solved, with the Bean's Ice Carrier.

Introduced to the L.L.Bean catalog in fall 1944, the Ice Carrier was constructed of heavy, oatmeal-colored canvas and riveted where the handles met the lip of the bag. A double layer of canvas on the base added an extra measure of resistance to abrasion and helped keep meltwater in its place. Such a stalwart bag practically begged for extra duty, perhaps, as L.L. helpfully suggested, "as a basket for wood, garden vegetables, fruit, etc." But for reasons unknown, the Ice Carrier's career was short-lived. Was that due to wartime supply disruptions? Poor sales? L.L. left no paper trail of his decision-making. By spring 1945 the canvas bag was gone from Bean's roster.

Twenty years passed before the Ice Carrier reemerged in summer 1965. It was the same concept, but with crucial modifications and a new name. Now the Boat and Tote, it was taller and more slender than its predecessor. The canvas was whiter and, in a masterstroke, the handles and base were colorized in nautical red or blue.

Proving you can't keep a good idea down, the Boat and Tote became a hit. In no time it was showing up everywhere in coastal New England and beyond. "It quickly became a symbol of the preppy class," observes Chris Hogan, menswear consultant and founder/editor-in-chief of the website Off the Cuff. "As others began to emulate this crowd, the Boat and Tote became a status symbol of the seaside life. In true preppy fashion, you never wanted one that looked too new. The more abuse it suffered, the better it looked, and others would then assume you'd had the bag for decades."

Simple, functional, and good-looking, the Boat and Tote had all the hallmarks of a Bean classic. Tough as nails, too. "We just had a Boat and Tote returned by a customer. Guy ran over it with his snowblower," says Jack Samson, who manages manufacturing at the L.L.Bean factory in Brunswick, Maine, where the Boat and Tote is made along with the Bean Boot. "The Boat and Tote looked pretty bad, but it really wrecked his snowblower."

Boat and Totes are built of #4 duck, an ironclad U.S.-made material commonly used in conveyor belts. Seams are single-stitched with heavy-duty T69 thread. The process of making a Boat and Tote, once very labor-intensive, is now largely automated and requires just seven minutes of actual hand and machine time. Skilled seamstresses still sew the handles to the bag and the V-point of the bottom material to the side of the bag. Look for that V-point to tell an original L.L.Bean Boat and Tote from its many imitators. "That's our signature," says Samson.

Products, like companies themselves, have to continually be updated and adapted as market conditions warrant. Rigidity is not an option, at least not for long. So it has been with the Boat and Tote since its inception. This simple bag's transformation reveals in miniature two of the major trends that swept consumer culture during the same time span: greater variety and personalization. That oatmeal-colored hauler of the 1940s was by 1995 transformed into a diverse product line including four sizes, three colors, two models (zip-top and open-top), and monogramming. Seasonal color choices were

The Ice Carrier, later renamed the Boat and Tote, was originally intended for carrying blocks of ice from distributors like the men pictured opposite.

Bean's Ice Carrier

This carrier is offered for those who have found difficulty in carrying ice from car to ice chest. A strong bag of builders' canvas that serves as a basket for wood, garden vegetables, fruit etc.

Size 10″ x 15″ on bottom. 13″ high.

Price $3.00 postpaid.

Bean's Men's Ski Pants

Made from a fine count 60% wool gabardine. Cut on the new instructor pattern which is acknowledged to be the most comfortable and stylish. Absolutely assures freedom of action. High waisted with wide belt loops. Pleated front. Equipped with elastic strap to pass under instep. Two tab pockets with button closing. One back pocket with

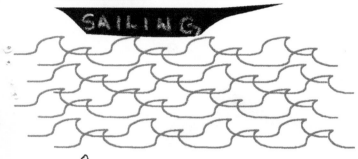

**YOU'RE BORN
YOU SAIL,
YOU DIE.**

Dear folks at LLBean...

Well, I could send this bag to the warranty department and say it didnt hold up... 😊 But its been a great bag and too old to figure out. I showed this photo to Jerry Havican, my reason for being a 'Beaner', he laughed and said I should show you...

So, thanks for your great bags. It was lucky to stand y for photo, sporting its new handles and Big Stuff Only written to keep small tools from falling out holes, which is good for now 😊

I have others in better shape... but just cant depart with a perfectly good bag.

thanks.

100 YEARS OF TOTING

HANDSOME, STRAIGHTFORWARD, AND IN IT FOR THE
LONG HAUL, WHEN IT COMES TO THE L.L.BEAN BOAT AND TOTE,
ITS MANY FANS GET A LITTLE CARRIED AWAY.

"I work at a preschool in Massachusetts, and we like the children to have school bags with handles. We thought you might appreciate knowing how much your bags are loved!"

—Karen C., Greenbush, Massachusetts, October 17, 2003

"I couldn't resist showing you another fantastic use of your Boat and Tote. My son Wyatt really enjoys sitting inside and watching the world go by."

—V.M., Rockville, Maryland, October 27, 2005

An Ode to Janet's Bean Bag

"There once was a bag made in Maine,
Straps of color, but otherwise plain.
Full of schoolbooks, wet clothes,
 mittens, towels, who knows?
Carried for years through sun, snow,
 and rain.

The bag was a gift in my youth,
At my side still as I'm long in the
 tooth.
Been out west and to Maine, to
 Virginia and Spain,
Plus a couple of trips to Duluth.

This bag has been at my side
Through thick and thin, taking
 everything in stride.

Outlasted two degrees, three jobs,
 a couple of pets, and a marriage,
It certainly has been one heck
 of a ride."

—Janet S., May 25, 2006

"I wanted to share with you two very special pictures. These pictures are of my first day of school, both as a student in 1990 and as a teacher in 2001. As you can see, L.L.Bean has been and still is with me through every step of my education. I truly appreciate the wonderful products you make and will continue to be a 'Beaner' fan for life."

—E.W., Arlington, Virginia, January 8, 2008

Bean, Me.

by W. F. LAWRENCE

Down-East Bonanza

Q. What do Bernard Baruch, Myrna Loy, Ernest Hemingway, Ted Williams, the Biddles, the Roosevelts, the du Ponts, and the King of Afghanistan have in common—besides money?

A. L.L. Bean, burly, booming-voiced, 88-year-old patriarch of the American sporting-goods business, mail-order mes-

Maine's Bean: It started with sore feet

siah to the discriminating sportsman for half-a-century.

And others, too, lean on Bean. Next week, L.L. Bean, Inc., will mail out more than 400,000 copies of its biannual catch-as-catch-can catalogue in anticipation of a 1961 gross of nearly $2.5 million—another record.

the "Maine Hunting Shoe," an immediate success and backbone to this day of the Bean business.

Bean later added a complete line of sporting goods ranging from snowshoes to duck decoys with the firm manufacturing more than half of the goods it sells —many the products of his personal "research and development" (i.e., hunting, fishing, and camping experience) in the North woods. Bean's outdoor laboratory produced, for instance, the Bean "Toter and Deer Carrier" (a stretcher-like device that is pushed along on one wheel), a coat without sleeves, a vest with sleeves, and a fur-lined bottle holder (to keep bottles from breaking under rough handling).

Money Magic: Bean's catalogue now lists more than 400 items, but it has no index. The Bean store itself is equally mystifying. It originally occupied the second floor over the village post office, but as Bean needed more space, he simply added a floor here, and a wing there and the store's 65,000 square feet now spill over onto nearly a dozen different interconnecting levels.

There is Yankee method, however, to the apparent madness. Bean omits the index from his catalogue because he figures each page is worth $10,000 in sales and he doesn't want to waste the space. Customers searching for one item in the catalogue, moreover, are lured by others en route; one Texan simply ordered "everything on pages 8 through 64." And for all the informality (Bean has no door on his office, just bellows when he wants someone), most orders are shipped out the day they are re-

■ IF YOU DON'T KNOW WHO L. L. Bean is, it's no crime—except in Freeport, Maine. But if you don't, chances are you are not a fisherman, hunter, hiker, or outdoorsman of any kind. In that event, it might appear curious to you that thousands of people— hundreds of thousands, in fact—drop

There's
man alive
catalog qu
to one of
flies. And
if trout do
flies, they'r
Yet a ma

Fortune

January 1955

It Takes a Sportsman

Next to Montgomery Ward's Sewell Avery, the best-known person in the U.S. mail-order business is probably Leon Leonwood ("L.L.") Bean, sporting-goods merchant of Freeport, Maine. Like Avery, Bean is in his early eighties, runs his company with a firm hand, and is a staunchly conservative man of business. His company earned $80,000 before taxes last year on $2 million worth of sales, and it owes not a cent to anybody.

Unlike Avery, Bean personally designs over half of his products,

have been sold and the item is still Bean's best seller.

The tremendous success of the Hunting Shoe convinced Bean that "it takes a sportsman to design equipment for sportsmen." Drawing on his camping knowledge, he began to increase his line of home-made specialties. He employed local townswomen to knit extra-length hunting socks and line them with fleece; he devised moccasins that would be impervious to stones, scarlet caps and capes to prevent shooting accidents, and a stretcher attached to

L. BEAN, of old Maine store fame, shook head: "I am an Atlantic salmon man."

JUSTICE William O. Douglas rattled his per and said: "I fish for *smallmouth* bas

"There's a fellow named Arnold

himself bounded up the stairs, tall a

The Boat and Tote Bag at the stitcher's station in the manufacturing plant. "We can't get them on the shelves fast enough."

soon added, then longer handles. In 2005 came the biggest change: customizable colors. For an extra fee, Bean customers could choose from no fewer than ten color options in the body, straps, bottom, pocket, and gusset (zip-top only), to create infinite variety and personal style.

Customization had immediate impact at the Brunswick factory. From an average of 500,000 bags made annually, production soared to a high-water mark of 1.2 million bags in 2007 (the year both Oprah Winfrey and Martha Stewart listed customizable Boat and Totes as among their favorite things). Few of these colorful, customized Boat and Totes will ever carry a block

of solid ice, but it's a fair bet quite a few will still be in service when L.L.Bean celebrates its 125th anniversary in 2037. "Boat and Totes don't wear out," says Samson. "They get downgraded to dirtier and dirtier jobs until they end up holding tire chains in the trunk."

....

If anyone alive in the early 1960s had yet to hear of L.L. Bean, the man and the company, they either lived under a rock or in a log cabin in

Opposite: Flattering news stories in the 1950s and 1960s strengthened L.L.'s already solid reputation. Above: A 1981 Maine newspaper touts the enduring popularity of the Boat and Tote.

TORTURE CHAMBER

BEFORE ANY PRODUCT OR MATERIAL WEARS THE L.L.BEAN LABEL, IT FIRST MUST WITHSTAND A HEAP OF ABUSIVE TREATMENT IN THE LABORATORY AND FIELD. ONLY THE STRONG SURVIVE.

The flat, pebbled roof of the Taylor Building in Freeport would seem an odd place for a campout. But there you'll find tents, a hammock, Adirondack chairs, and an outdoor end table set up for months at a time. No weenies or s'mores will be roasted up here, although the temperature of the roof deck on a hot summer afternoon could probably accomplish that. You're witnessing a product test conducted in slow motion, where the action of sun, wind, rain, and temperature extremes on the outdoor equipment is being minutely calibrated.

Above, left to right: A Bean boot is submerged; a waterproof-treated sweatshirt takes a shower; luggage is repeatedly thrown down two stair flights; a bookpack's shoulder straps are tugged with great force.

Backed by five full-time testing technicians, a 4,000-square-foot state-of-the-art laboratory, and a battalion of 1,200 testers in the field from Alaska to Costa Rica, L.L.Bean leads the industry in ripping, pulling, dousing, baking, freezing, flexing, pressurizing, abrading, smashing, washing, drying, and generally torturing materials. It all started with L.L. himself, who assured customers he tested every product in the field before placing it on the market.

Bean's testing got seriously scientific in 1985, when the new testing lab in Freeport opened. Today it's staffed by materials experts and led by Dave DaPonte. "The one thing you don't want is your customer to be your tester," says DaPonte.

Any material that's new to Bean must first be proven to work as advertised. "We want to know: is it going to perform, is it durable, and are there any safety issues?" says DaPonte. Specialized machines put products to the test. Buttons get smashed by dropped weights. Cotton fabric is punctured, then ripped by a pendulum device that measures resistance to tearing. Knit wool is rubbed repeatedly to check for pilling. Boot leather is flexed 500,000 times.

Candleholders are checked for overheating. Zippers are zipped 20,000 times. Waterproof material is shot with a stream of water pressurized at thirty pounds per square inch for sixty seconds. Paint is zapped by an XRF gun that tests for lead and arsenic.

Approved materials enter a library from which product designers and developers can choose. But testing doesn't end there. Just because a shirt or waterproof wader is assembled from approved materials doesn't mean the finished product passes. The waterproof seams on that wader are bombarded by water under increasing pressure until the failure point is established. Button attachments on a kid's shirt are yanked at by twenty-one pounds of force for ten seconds (ten samples each of every cuff button, pocket button, and front button). "One failure and it's back to the drawing board," says Dan Otis, a product-safety and material analyst.

If a product has made it through the in-house testing, then it's shipped to field testers for careful observation under real-world conditions found on the glaciers of Washington State or salmon streams in New Brunswick.

It's an exhaustive process but absolutely necessary when a

company stakes an unconditional guarantee and its reputation on everything it sells. The test team pits Bean products against their competitors to make sure they are market leaders. In 2009 the latest, greatest thing in winter jackets was battery-powered heating, which was being carried by other top outdoor brands but was rejected by the L.L.Bean testing team because the batteries overheated. Sure enough, the technology was soon pulled from other companies' shelves because of similar complaints.

After a product is released for sale, the test team continues to monitor its performance via customer feedback online and in the mail. In 2011, when customer reviews on the website complained that a waterproof breathable jacket was leaving them wet in the rain, the test team got to work. "We knew the fabric and seams had passed our tests, so I put the jacket on a mannequin in the shower unit," says Otis. "When cinched tight, the elastic drawstrings on the hood created channels for water to slide right down the neckline. We got the design and product teams in here to see what was happening. The problem got fixed right away."

Top to bottom: Shipping room, Christmas 1961; opening mail orders, 1962 (left to right: Eunice Pitts, Thelma Sommers, Idalyn Cummings, Helen Stilkey, Mary Dyer); the back of a 1956 postcard read: "Sorry we don't have the exact address however have heard much of your sporting goods. Please forward catalog."

the Alaskan wilderness. (Even the latter excuse couldn't guarantee ignorance of the mail-order merchant from Maine, because Alaska was one of the company's best markets. Orders from the Alaskan bush arrived in Freeport in predictable spurts timed several days after the mail boat from Alaska docked in Seattle.) L.L.'s reputation grew far and wide during the 1950s thanks to a series of glowing profiles in publications as diverse as *Sports Illustrated*, *The New Yorker*, *Down East*, *Forbes*, *Sports Afield*, *Reader's Digest*, and *Coronet*. There would be no more "discovering" L.L.Bean; the company and its originator were household names.

The writers of those stories invariably were charmed by L.L. and his "Horatio Alger of the Maine woods" biography, but in their printed work was a persistent theme of wonderment at the increasingly outmoded arrangement of the L.L.Bean factory and store. Yankee ingenuity and a spirit of making do gave the enterprise an internal logic but one that simply befuddled outsiders. "It looks like a cross between Grandma's attic and a broken roller coaster," said a *Time* magazine reporter of the factory store in 1962. "Organized chaos," was the descriptive a book author used. So disorienting was the factory store's maze of rooms, ramps, and corridors that employees liked to tell the story of one slightly inebriated late-night customer who became hopelessly lost. He was found the next morning dozing under an overturned stack of hunting pants.

Orders continued to flow into the L.L.Bean offices by the bagful, new products issued forth at regular intervals, and the catalog grew both in size and in the number of copies mailed. The business climate couldn't have been riper for an outdoor-products specialist. Americans were flush with cash and free time—the length of the average workweek during the mid-1950s having shrunk to the lowest level at any point before or since—and they were taking to the woods and

THE CUSTOMER IS ALWAYS RIGHT. USUALLY.

The three thousand customer-care representatives in Maine who answer L.L.Bean's 1-800 hotline take pride in delivering the best service in the business. (L.L.Bean, Inc. was voted #1 in 2010 by *BusinessWeek*.) Reps handle up to one hundred calls in a day, each one presenting an opportunity to make good on L.L.'s pledge of 100 percent customer satisfaction. And every now and then, a call offers an opportunity for a good chuckle. Bean customer reps recall some of their funnier conversations:

Customer: "I'd like to order an XL dog bed."
Rep: "Of course. Would you like this monogrammed?"
Customer: "No—my dog can't read!"

Customer: "'Where's my check?"
Rep: "Your check for what, sir?"
Customer: "I returned my old Bean boots to have them 'resold.' I'm expecting a check for their value after L.L.Bean sold them."

Rep: "Hello, L.L.Bean, can I help you?"
Customer (an elderly woman): "Ella Bean, again! I get you every time I call!"

Customer (calling from New York City): "I'm refusing delivery on the canoe I ordered."
Rep: "Why is that, ma'am?"
Customer: "It won't fit in my elevator."

Customer: "How much does that air mattress weigh?"
Rep: "Three pounds."
Customer: "How about when it's full?"

Customer: "Do you sell Orvis hats?"
Rep: "No, we don't."
Customer: "Where can I buy an Orvis hat?"
Rep: "I'd try Orvis."
Customer: "Who's Orvis? Never heard of them."

Customer: "I'm very disappointed with the Christmas wreath I purchased last year."
Rep: "I'm sorry. What seems to have been wrong with it?"
Customer: "I put it away in the attic, and now all the needles are brown and falling off. I won't be able to use it again for another Christmas."

AMERICANS WERE FLUSH WIT[H]
THEY WERE TAKIN[G]

CASH AND FREE TIME, AND
TO THE WOODS AND STREAMS

streams. The number of licensed hunters and fishermen reached an all-time high, and family camping was immensely popular. Clearly a lot was going right. Or was it?

A fresh set of eyes was closely observing the company's operations from the inside: Leon Gorman, L.L.'s grandson through his daughter Barbara, was honorably discharged by the U.S. Navy in summer 1960, when he was hired at L.L.Bean as a clothing buyer at eighty dollars a week. Leon was never certain whether his grandfather took him in because of the sharp cut of the Navy uniform he wore to the interview, his college degree, or a sense of family obligation. Leon's duties were vague, so he gravitated to the salesroom. He waited on customers and learned everything he could about the company and its products.

Leon had little knowledge of management theory or business organization at the time, but he could tell that L.L.Bean was adrift. His grandfather was eighty-seven years old and stuck in his ways. A vacation home in Pompano Beach, Florida, and the pursuit of feisty sailfish absorbed more of L.L.'s attention by the year. All new product ideas and catalog copy had to wait on L.L.'s return to the office for his approval. Neither L.L. nor his son Carl, who ran the place in his absence, cared much for change. "Everything had to be done more or less as it had been the year before, or the company would lose its equilibrium," wrote Leon years later in his book about the company, *L.L.Bean: The Making of an American Icon*.

"During the '50s and early '60s, L.L.'s company was suffering from a lack of management and direction. His product groups were right, but the specific products were getting out of date and there were lapses in quality. Service was becoming erratic and the catalogs and advertisements were repetitive and losing their effectiveness." Everywhere Leon looked were warning signs. Other businesses were

L.L.Bean, Inc. directors meet in 1962 (left to right: Tom Gorman, L.L., Warren Bean, Carl Bean, and Leon Gorman).

GOING THE EXTRA MILE

IN LITTLE WAYS AND BIG, L.L.BEAN'S RETAIL-SALES AND CUSTOMER-CARE REPS HAVE ALWAYS GONE THE EXTRA MILE TO SATISFY CUSTOMERS:

SPECIAL DELIVERY

While serving as a sales rep in the retail store in the early 1980s, Ed Dwyer sold a camping stove to a woman who was going to Ireland. What transpired next adds new meaning to the phrase "no sale is final." "She had no sooner left the store than I realized she could have difficulty locating the proper fuel in Ireland," said Dwyer. "I was concerned about this and went to the cashier and found that she had paid with a check that listed a town in Vermont as the only address. The next day, with a more appropriate backpacking stove in hand (it was my day off, Sunday), I drove to the small town in Vermont, went to the general store, and was given directions to the customer's house. I found the woman, exchanged stoves, and instructed her in how to use it. It was a beautiful Sunday trek for me—and the postcards I received from Ireland confirmed the fact that L.L.Bean had another satisfied customer."

AUTUMN BLUES

A customer-care rep took a phone order from an older gentleman who had relocated to Florida from New York State. They got to talking about the fine autumn weather in Freeport. "How I miss fall up north," he said. On her lunch break, the rep found a glowing red sugar-maple leaf and sent it overnight to a homesick New Yorker.

SEASONAL HELP

A customer called the 800 number to find out how to season her new cast-iron cookware. But L.L.Bean didn't sell cast-iron cookware at the time, so she must have purchased it from another retailer. The customer's friend told her to call L.L.Bean, since "they know everything!" The phone rep, who knew her way around a kitchen, told the caller how to use oil to season the cookware, and she hung up a happy (potential) customer.

SANTA'S HELPER

"I was born in 1945, so my story is from the early '50s, when we would travel to our summer home on Sebec Lake from Virginia," says customer Chris Balsley. "It took several days because there were no turnpikes back then. We traveled at night so my brother and I would be asleep in the backseat, and not roughhousing. We would wake up in Dover, Maine, with new L.L.Bean Moccasins on our feet. We thought that Santa had magically put them on us. Little did we know that Dad had driven by L.L.Bean (then a tiny store) and had a salesman come out, measure our feet, and put new mocs on us. It seems that customer service has always been important in Freeport."

BIG-BOX RETAILING

A young woman who worked at the retail store saw a big package fall off the roof rack of a bright red Chevy station wagon. The box bore no identifying label. So she put it in her car and spent her lunch hour driving around Freeport on the chance the driver hadn't left town. She spotted the red station wagon outside a popular restaurant and had the manager page its owner. The young employee declined the owner's offer of a twenty-dollar bill but gladly accepted his thanks. "I couldn't have this man thinking his package was stolen in Bean's parking lot!" she said.

MANY HAPPY RETURNS

With L.L.Bean's no-questions-asked guarantee, returns department employees never know what the next box might contain. A few surprising discoveries:
- False teeth found in a bathrobe pocket
- A live gecko that stowed away in a package from Baton Rouge, Louisiana
- $7,000 cash stuffed in the toe of a Bean Boot sent for resoling (promptly returned to a very happy customer!)

LOST-AND-FOUND DEPARTMENT

A story published in *Redbook* told of an unusual phone call L.L.Bean customer-care rep Loretta Greene received on November 1, 1992. On the other end of the line was police officer Frank Montalbano of Staten Island, New York. Two officers from his department had found a dazed elderly woman wandering the streets in the middle of the night clutching a small terrier. The woman could not remember her name, address, or any other personal details. The dog's tags, however, read, "My name is Tiger. Please return to Mary Will, Bethesda, Maryland." A call to information found no such listing. Officer Montalbano noticed the woman wore an L.L.Bean watch. Perhaps L.L.Bean could help find a phone number or address?

Greene informed Montalbano of the company's strict policy protecting customer confidentiality. But she was moved by the officer's frustration and learned the woman would be sent to a shelter if relatives couldn't be located. Greene punched in zip codes around Staten Island. No luck. She tried zip codes in and around Bethesda, and up came a Mary Will whose last order had been a small dog bed and a field watch.

"Does she have a very small dog?" asked Greene. "Is the watch a field one?" Yes on both. Greene figured the woman might live alone, so she checked Mary's order history to see if she'd sent gifts to relatives. She had.

Montalbano made a call to Albert Will of Yardley, Pennsylvania, whose seventy-eight-year-old mother had set off the day before to come visit. When she never showed, Albert notified police departments and hospitals, and retraced his mother's route, checking every rest stop. Within two hours, Albert and his mother were reunited. A doctor's examination revealed that Mary had suffered temporary memory loss, from which she recovered. "Without Loretta, this woman might not have seen her family again," said Montalbano.

"THE WAY I LOOK AT IT, NOBODY EVER WON AN ARGUMENT WITH A CUSTOMER." – L.L. BEAN

streamlining with new electronic record keeping and rudimentary computers, but at Bean customer records were still being kept on three-by-five-inch cards, the mailing list was typewritten, and inventory management was nonexistent. The workforce (whose average age was in the mid-sixties) and physical plant were ready for retirement. "Overall, operations of the company were pretty much as they had been since the end of World War II," concluded Leon.

Sales had essentially flattened during the 1950s, if not regressed when factoring in inflation, and profit margins were razor-thin at 2 percent. Every suggestion made to L.L. for growing or altering the company met with the same shopworn reply: "I get three good meals a day, and I can't eat four." Like many entrepreneurs before him and since, L.L. had a difficult time delegating and letting go. This was no more apparent than with the company's most public face and L.L.'s pride and joy: the catalog.

From the beginning, the Bean catalog was one of a kind. L.L. wrote the copy in a personable, assured tone that stood out from the written-by-committee style of Sears, Roebuck and Co. and the other giant catalogers. His catalog's earnest presentation and haphazard organization—charming when the book was sixteen pages, less so as the catalog topped one hundred pages—were like the print version of a New England crossroads general store. On the same page of the spring 1955 catalog you could find a

Below left: Julian "Andy" Andrews and Leon Gorman look at snowshoes. Below right: Leon Gorman examines the spring 1969 catalog.

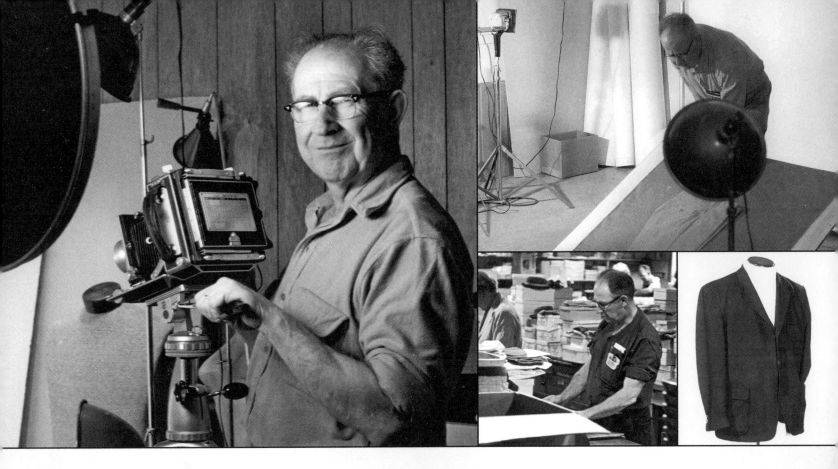

THE FACE OF BEAN: MEL COLLINS

L.L.'s words set the tone for the Bean catalog. Clifford "Mel" Collins's photos gave it a distinct look. From 1945 to 1949 and again from 1955 to 1974, Collins photographed almost every item to appear in the catalog. L.L. sold it straight, and Collins shot it straight. "Never used fancy setups or airbrushed anything, so there was lots of credibility," said Leon Gorman in his book *L.L. Bean: The Making of an American Icon.*

Collins's first studio was a small, low-ceilinged room downstairs at the old L.L.Bean factory near the maintenance department. "Every time the leather cutter upstairs came down, the dust would come down, and if you [were shooting] a white shirt, it was a sight!" he said. Contrast that arrangement with today's 16,000 square-foot Studio 1912 in Westbrook, Maine, where teams of photographers and stylists prepare photos for today's catalogs and website.

Collins's unadorned photos—with items always shown in silhouette—suited the neat, practical products Bean sold at the time. When models started to appear in the catalog, they were L.L. Bean employees shot by Collins to earnest or comic effect, depending on your point of view. "The model looks like the madman who installed the plumbing at your cottage, or the guy who sold you the camper," noted a 1972 article in *Sports Illustrated.* "It is sort of democratic catalog élan."

Collins wore several hats at Bean, including clothing buyer and L.L.'s longtime assistant, before settling into the house photographer's role. In fact, it was Collins who taught Leon the company's very basic inventory system during his first weeks on the job. Collins died at age eighty-seven in 1996.

Above left: Clifford "Mel" Collins in his studio, 1971.
Top right: Collins adjusts a pair of chino shorts.
Above right: Collins's old jacket, shot at his new studio in the Taylor Building on Casco Street in Freeport, 1971.
Above middle: Mel Collins in the shipping-and-packing room, 1962.

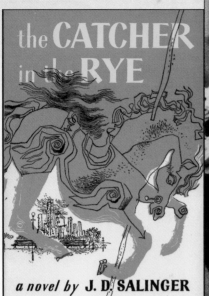

The Catcher in the Rye **published**

24/7/365: L.L. Bean retail store opens 'round the clock

Route 1 bypass goes around Freeport

1954

1951

Ladies' Department opens at retail store

Elvis Presley's "Heartbreak Hotel" goes gold

1957

1956

1960

L.L. publishes autobiography, *My Story: The Autobiography of a Down-East Merchant*

Baseball star Ted Williams offers to buy L.L.Bean

Leon Gorman, future president, hired at eighty dollars a week

Soviets launch Sputnik

I Love Lucy finishes six-year run

JFK assassinated; retail store closes for second time. (The blue laws caused the first temporary closing.)

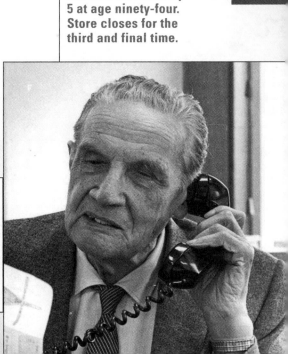

First U.S. combat troops arrive in Vietnam

Memorial Arch completed in St. Louis

Muhammad Ali upsets Sonny Liston in Lewiston, Maine

1961

1964

1967

1951–1967

1963

1965

L.L. dies on February 5 at age ninety-four. Store closes for the third and final time.

Ka-ching: Employees get bonus equal to 30 percent of wages

Berlin Wall erected

Bean sells its first Down Filled Sleeping Bag

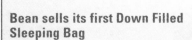

Down Filled Sleeping Bag

Weight 8½ lbs.   Finished size 33″ x 76″.   Color, Olive.
Price, in poplin duffle bag, $58.75 postpaid.

The '60s produced two style icons whose indelible mark on fashion is indisputable: actress Audrey Hepburn and First Lady Jacqueline Kennedy. Every woman wanted to look like them—simultaneously elegant, refined, and feminine—and while the ladies' stellar genetics proved unattainable, any woman could buy a dress featuring the hallmarks of chic: simple lines, a raised hemline, and a ladylike silhouette. More Camelot than backlot, L.L.Bean offered this Cape-ready cotton print dress. Just add (well-worn) Boat and Tote.

Bean's Shirt Dress

This '60s take on the fashion staple known as the shirt dress, or shirtwaist dress, never appeared in the Bean catalog; it was a retail-only item when the women's department started growing in the '60s.

Signature details like cuffed sleeves, front buttons, and a cinched waistline made it classic.

A hemline above the knee and an abstract print made it current but still demure.

L.L.Bean Staff Model: Katie Pulsifer Martin

Years at Bean: 10
Hobbies: Ice dancing
Accomplishments: "I am learning how to surf and love all things related to the ocean, especially my wooden boat (*Scout*) that I helped build with my father (he is a local boat builder)."
Favorite Bean Product: "My Signature Zippered Duffle in solid black, a replica of a design from 1934."

Sheepskin Rug, Ladies' Field Slacks, Ladies' Hand Sewed Loungers, and Feathered Bass Minnow. Whatever you needed could be found in there somewhere. If not, just look harder.

There was method to the catalog's mayhem. "We use the printed page to prompt impulse sales," L.L. explained to a writer from *Sales Management* magazine in 1955. "For example, if a customer wants to see what we carry in the line of flies, the index tells him we feature 24 kinds. These are listed on 11 pages in the catalog. By the time he's seen our 24 flies, he's also looked at 62 other items on the same and facing pages. With this method, the customer finds a lot of things he's always wanted, things he'd like to try, and things he'll buy while he's filling out his mail order."

L.L. gradually relinquished copywriting and layout of the spring and fall catalogs to others but reserved ultimate editorial authority, which he wielded with a red pencil and a big "LLB: OK" stamp until the year he died (see page 57). His verve and decided point of view still permeated the catalog but were waning. In Leon's mind, the impulse-buying theory behind the catalog format was a rationalization for an outdated mishmash. Confronting L.L. about weaknesses in the catalog and product lines was fruitless, so Leon's strategy was to work around his grandfather. He convinced L.L. of the need for a thirty-two-page circular timed for Christmas 1963. Since L.L. didn't pay much attention to circulars, this proved the ideal vehicle to test new products that might eventually wind up in the all-important spring and fall catalogs. A summer circular soon followed.

"I suppose it was subterfuge," admitted Leon, "but all the products added to the catalog in this way had been proven via circular sales and in fact were not 'new.'"

On more than a few occasions Leon thought about leaving Bean and its frustrations for a

---

"Out of the Ordinary" Christmas Suggestions for 1963

Bean's Quilted Nylon Parka

An all purpose reversible parka. 100% nylon shell quilted in a five-inch diamond pattern with an eight ounce acryllic batting fill providing warmth without weight. Reverse side is smooth of contrasting color nylon. Body length 30". Self collar with roll type, drawstring hood, take-up tabs at the side, reversible two way zipper. Two vertical pockets on outside and one horizontal pocket on reverse side. Machine washable.
Colors: Black reversing to Scarlet.
       Taupe reversing to Putty Tan.
Men's sizes: Small, Medium, Large and Extra Large.

Price, $19.95 postpaid.

Safari Grill

Four double sheets of newspaper, tightly rolled, will broil meats or fowl in 5 to 10 minutes. Very little smoke and almost no residue.
Grill is heavy gauge steel with baked enamel finish. Nickel plated grid has handle that does not heat up. Measures 13" high by 12½" in diameter. Three parts nest into handy carrying case.

Price, $10.95 postpaid.

Cold Weather Ankle Boot

A lightweight two-eyelet ankle boot made with genuine sheepskin lining. Soft upper leather with non-slip crepe soles and heels. Ideal for cold weather wear and for use as an after ski boot.
Color, Brown.
Men's sizes 7 to 13, whole and half sizes. (No size 12½). Two widths, Medium and Wide.

Price, $14.80 postpaid.

Gift Certificate

Most Hunters and Fishermen prefer to select their own equipment.
Merchandise Gift Certificates are available in any specified amount. Send us your check and we will immediately send you, or any person you specify, a Certificate which entitles Bearer to merchandise equal to amount of Certificate. A Fall Catalog will be sent at same time from which to select goods.

L. L. Bean, Inc. Freeport, Me.

Bean's 1966 Summer Circular

Maine
Gloucester Harbor-Hampton
Massachusetts Bay
Cape Cod
Narragansett Bay
New York-Long Island
Northern Jersey

Bean's Brushed Denim Shirt

Fabric is the popular "Scrubdenim", a sturdy cotton denim with a soft, sueded finish. Unusually comfortable and long wearing it makes into a handsome and very useful shirt. Sanforized® for washability.
Long sleeves and tails, two flapped pockets and anchor buttons. Doubles as a jacket and worn by men and ladies.
Color, Faded Blue.
Sizes: Extra Small, Small, Medium, Large and Extra Large.
Price, $8.90 postpaid. Send for free sample.

Navigation Chart Place Mats

Regulation charts in standard navigation colors. Sealed in high quality polyethylene plastic for use as table place mats. Indestructible and easily cleaned. Fourteen charts covering the following areas:
Chesapeake Bay
Cape Hatteras
Florida
Erie-Ontario
Lake Superior
Michigan-Huron
San Francisco and Coast

Price, 95c each. Four for $3.45 postpaid.

"Sperry Top-Sider" Oxford
(For Men and Women)

Features the famous Squeegee Sole. Extra thick rubber with razor-fine, zig-zag cuts that will not slip on wet or dry surfaces. Also very flexible.
High grade canvas with non-chafe lining and heel cushion. Contoured fit. Will outwear several ordinary pairs of canvas shoes.
For boating and active sports. Handsome enough for general leisure wear. Now available in two colors: White, Blue.
Ladies' sizes 4 to 10. Narrow or Medium width. $9.95 postpaid.
Men's sizes 6 to 13. (No size 12½.) Medium width. $9.95 postpaid.

Boat and Tote Bag

A handy tote bag for the boater or camper. Sturdily constructed from extra heavy white duck.
While designed to carry ice, its large capacity is very useful in carrying and protecting bulky and odd shaped gear or clothing. Keeps them out of the way but instantly available.
Two colors: White with Red trim. White with Blue trim.
Size 8" x 17" x 16" high.
Price, $4.75 postpaid.

L. L. Bean, Inc. Freeport, Me.

In the 1960s, Leon Gorman persuaded L.L. to allow Christmas and summer circulars. The company used these off-peak mailings to test out new products for the spring and fall catalogs.

OUT OF RESPECT TO LEON L. BEAN PRESIDENT WE WILL BE CLOSED THURSDAY FEBRUARY 9th

more exciting career, but the potential of the place fascinated him. "I liked the idea of L.L.Bean and the way of life its products represented. L.L.'s Golden Rule of treating customers like human beings made a lot of sense," said Leon. "I liked the customers I had met in the store and those who corresponded with us by mail. L.L.'s notions of 'good merchandise,' although lacking in execution at the time, influenced me a lot. I also liked the people who worked at L.L.Bean and their sincere and helpful attitudes.

"I had no grand plans for the company," continued Leon, "but I saw many opportunities to do a better job for our customers and for Bean people."

Leon's modifications to the catalog soon began paying dividends. By 1967 sales were twice those of 1960 on the strength of a product assortment that was 75 percent new. The mailing list had grown from 350,000 to 600,000. Intrigued by the turnaround at L.L.Bean and the textbook clash of managerial and business philosophies between Leon and the old guard, the Harvard

Business School presented the company's situation in one of its vaunted case studies. "Leon Arthur Gorman wondered if his grandfather's philosophy and business methods could be incorporated into new management systems," summed the study, "or whether there would have to be important changes to enable the company to continue its profitable growth."

Leon was attending a sporting-goods trade show in Chicago when he received news long anticipated but unfathomable nonetheless. The unstoppable Leon Leonwood Bean—by his own description "the world-famous Yankee hunter and fisherman [who] turned his love of outdoor life into a multimillion-dollar success story"— had died peacefully on February 5, 1967, at the age of ninety-four. L.L.'s funeral would close the Freeport retail store for only the third time since 24/7 operation began in 1951 (the day of John F. Kennedy's assassination was the second). When the doors reopened, Leon, his coworkers, and L.L.Bean's customers would find out whether the company could survive without its living symbol.

Above: Sign from the retail store announcing closing due to L.L.'s death on February 5, 1967. Opposite: L.L. with a tuna in Palm Beach Shores, Florida, in the late '50s.

CHAPTER 5

BACK TO NATURE

| *The* **GOOSE DOWN VEST** | First sold in **1971** |

THERE'S NO TELLING WHAT L.L. WOULD HAVE THOUGHT OF THE GOOSE DOWN VEST. DEBUTING IN 1971 AS THE TRAIL MODEL VEST, THIS LIGHTWEIGHT, DOWN-FILLED GARMENT WAS MEANT FOR A NEW BREED OF OUTDOOR ENTHUSIASTS—THE BACKPACKERS. THESE YOUNG PEOPLE LOOKED TO NATURE FOR PEACE AND TRANQUILLITY, AND L.L.BEAN WAS RIGHT THERE WITH THEM. HOME AND CAMP FURNISHINGS JOINED HUNTING GEAR IN THE CATALOG, AND IN 1980, SALES REACHED $121.5 MILLION.

You're in camp as balmy day gives way to chilly night. The location could be the Sierra Nevada in July or the Adirondacks in early September. Your flannel shirt isn't staving off the goose bumps. You need another layer, one that's warm and light and unrestrictive. And if it can be rolled up into a perfect backcountry pillow, all the better. A wool sweater could do the job but would be too bulky in the backpack. For just such an occasion was the Trail Model Vest designed in 1971.

The Trail Model Vest, priced at $23.50, was simplicity defined. Its outer shell of ripstop nylon repelled wind and rain. Quilted stitching joined inside panel to outside panel to create chambers that were filled with 3.5 ounces of "prime Northern Goose Down." No zipper (just front snaps), no pocket flaps, no special liner, nothing fancy. Its total weight and compressed size were about that of a softball. "It was really meant for the minimalist backpacker going extra-light and searching for weight and bulk reduction," says A.J. Curran, Bean's director of product for outerwear and accessories.

Backpackers were a new market for L.L.Bean. In fact, backpackers were a new market for practically every outdoor supplier, and for good reason: prior to 1970 they simply didn't exist. Except for a few misfit ramblers, every hiker returned to the trailhead at day's end. That all changed in a hurry. Ever-increasing numbers of young people began strapping on big, external-frame backpacks and venturing out into the wilderness. The instruments of their liberation were made of nylon and nature's miraculous insulator: down. Freed of burdensome canvas tents, wool outerwear, and cotton-pile sleeping bags, these wanderers ranged farther and in greater comfort than previously imagined possible.

Down is a perfect insulator. It doesn't produce heat but instead prevents heat loss. Each cluster's many thousands of filaments interlock with its neighbors' to trap air. The more air pockets, or loft, the greater the retention of body heat and your perception of warmth. Materials scientists have tried for some forty years to synthesize down's amazing properties. They've gotten close with man-made fibers but still can't replicate down's trifecta of high loft, light weight, and excellent compressibility.

What worked on the trail also worked on the street. By the mid-1970s, college campuses had a new uniform: flannel shirt, chunky leather boots, and the must-have down vest. The look said: "I might not ever hike the John Muir Trail or climb Longs Peak, but I could." Apparel pros like Curran call that shift from function to fashion "crossover value." The Trail Model Vest had it.

Trail Model Vest
(For Men and Women)

Filled with 3.5 ounces of prime Northern Goose Down. Warms the body over a wide range of temperatures. Shell fabric of wind resistant, water repellent "Ripstop" nylon. Ultra-light (only 9 oz.) with snap front, down collar and useful, self-closing pockets. Kidney warmer back, length about 26″ and packs compactly. Should go along on any camping, fishing or cold weather outing.

Two colors: Blue. Green.

Ladies' sizes: Small (30-32), Medium (34-36) and Large (38-40).

4238 Ladies' Trail Model Vest, $23.50 postpaid.

Men's sizes: Small (38), Medium (41), Large (44) and Extra Large (47).

1419 Men's Trail Model Vest, $23.50 postpaid.

Left: The Trail Model Vest in Bean's fall 1974 catalog—four years after its debut. Opposite: A grateful letter and photograph from a Bean fan.

Dear sir,

Enclosed is a photograph of my boy-friend and myself wearing your hollofil West Branch style vests. This picture was taken in upstate New York last winter. We both enjoyed wearing your vests and thought perhaps your advertising department might consider this photograph for the fall catalog. I will be happy to send the negative of this picture if you should decide to use it. Doing business with your company is a pleasure and we take great pride in wearing your merchandise.

L. L. Bean dies at age 94

FREEPORT — Leon L. Bean, 94, founder and president of L. L. Bean Inc., a sporting goods business which he started about 55 years ago and which is now world famous, died Sunday in a hospital at Pomano Beach, Fla. He was taken ill while vacationing at his winter home in Deerfield Beach, Fla.

He is survived by his second wife, the former Claire Boudreau of Belmont, Mass., whom he married in 1940; two sons, Lester Carl Bean and Charles Warren Bean, both of whom are associated with the family firm; a daughter, Mrs. John L. Gorman of Yarmouth; five grandchildren, six great-grandchildren, two nieces and two nephews. His first wife, the former Bertha Porter of Freeport, whom he married in 1898, died in 1939.

Funeral services will be held in Freeport at 2 p m. Thursday. The Rev. Leslie Craig of Dover-Foxcroft will officiate. Interment will be in Webster Cemetery, Freeport, in the spring.

Mr. Bean was born in Greenwood, Oct. 13, 1872, the son of Benjamin Warren and Sarah Swett Bean. Although his parents had died by the time he was 12 years of age, he determined to get some formal schooling. This decision started him on a super-salesman's career, as he sold soap to pay for his schooling, which included about a year at Kents Hill School, Readfield, and later a semester at Hebron Academy.

Ever an ardent outdoor sportsman, it was his enthusiasm for outdoor sports that started Leon Leonwood Bean on a business that has expanded so tremendously over the years; a firm whose store remains open 24 hours a day, 365 days a year; a business which sends out nearly a half million Bean catalogs; and in a half-century has grossed millions and employed more than 100 persons.

It was 55 years ago that Bean designed a hunting boot which he felt was better than any other at that time, his famous waterproof hunting boot which has been a best seller through the years although over 100 different kinds of shoes are manufactured by the firm today. He went into business for himself in 1912, backed by a $400 loan. With the advent of the new boot, he decided to publish a catalog for mailing for prospective customers. The first L.L. Bean catalog was published that year, and contained three pages.

Items were constantly added to the store's stock, the majority of them for sportsmen. Outdoor clothing, tents, stoves, cooking gear, boats and canoes, firearms, accessories, and all the other 1,001 articles needed to make life in the woods less primitive gradually found their places on the

L. L. BEAN

Bean shelves. Nearly every item was tested personally by Bean himself on his numerous hunting and fishing trips.

By 1937, when the firm celebrated its first quarter century, its business was grossing half a million dollars a year. The Freeport plant grew. Bean bought adjoining parcels of land and the rambling complex of multi-stories frame buildings expanded beyond the original store.

The Freeport post office, housed formerly in the Bean establishment, grew along with the company, and has been a first-class one for many years now due to the Bean mail-order business. In some years the business has accounted for more than 80 per cent of the post office's volume. The store has become so famous that letters addressed only "Bean, Maine," have found their way to Freeport.

The catalog goes to sportsmen all over the world twice a year. It is widely admired in a civilization which deals in superlatives and streamlining. Its prose is sparse and laconic in a Yankee way, and its illustrations are mostly unretouched photographs.

A good many items of Bean merchandise are made in the local plant. Several years ago Mrs. Bean acquired Small & Abbott, shoe manufactures, and this subsidiary plant turns out moccasins and other sporting footgear. Another item is fishing flies and many Freeport women have been engaged in this work.

The fall of 1960 was doubly noteworthy in the long, successful life of "double-L" Bean, when he announced: (1) A record press run for his fall catalog; and (2) The publication of his autobiography — "My Story," by L. L. Bean. The book also included many pictures, photographs of Mr. Bean, his family, his possessions, and his trophies. It also had reprints of letters from many great men, including presidents. Included too was a reprint of a letter addressed to The Brunswick Record in July, 1938, in which the writer, A. P. Winslow, asked for improved conditions at the Freeport post office. A high point in the book, the writing of L. L. himself, says, "For years all our profits were spent in advertising. The results have proved our judgement was correct."

Mr. Bean held numerous memberships, many of them honorary, in sporting organizations. He had been a Freeport selectman and member of the town's budget committee. During the "depression" years, as president of the Freeport Realty Co., he was instrumental in bringing several new businesses to Freeport. He was a past master and a member for nearly 60 years of Freeport Lodge, No. 23, AF & AM, which will hold Masonic memorial services Thursday at the funeral.

Opposite: *Times-Record* obituary, page 12, Monday, February 6, 1967. Left: NBC's Chet Huntley announces the death of L.L. on February 5, 1967. Pages 128–129: Condolence letters poured in after L.L.'s passing.

Today, the Trail Model Vest is gone from the Bean catalog, but its spirit lives in the Goose Down Vest ($59). With more extras than its predecessor—zippers on the front and side pockets, an unquilted nylon taffeta interior lining that moves easily over bottom layers and acts as a windbreaker—the Goose Down Vest still manages similar warmth at roughly the same weight, due to the use of high-grade 650 fill goose down. "The Goose Down Vest is a great example of a garment that takes into account what we've learned through the years and offers the best combination of features, benefits, and value," says Maynard McCorkle, a materials specialist at L.L.Bean.

....

Word of Leon Leonwood Bean's death met with sadness and uncertainty in the Bean factory and among the customer base. "To say that this was the passing of a patriarch and...the passing of an era is to understate the matter considerably," wrote longtime Bean employee Carlene Griffin. "L.L. *was* the company—and I know of no employee who didn't have tears in his or her eyes when the solemn news of L.L.'s death came to us."

In the national media, L.L.'s passing was treated with prominence. Hundreds of newspapers carried his obituary. *Time* magazine hailed him as the "Merchant of the Maine Woods," and credited the nonagenarian with working right up to the end reading galley proofs of the spring 1967 catalog that would mail the day after his funeral. NBC's evening news program, *The Huntley-Brinkley Report*, devoted eight minutes of airtime to L.L.'s obituary. L.L. had clearly transcended the boundaries of his catalog business to become a beloved public figure. Some 50,000 condolence letters poured into the company. Many asked for a copy of the spring catalog, which surely would have pleased an old merchandiser who prized free advertising.

"L.L.'s death was a traumatic moment for

Very recently ... a TV program — concerning your company — and the passing away of Mr. Bean, the founder of your business — I was glad to hear that his sons + grandchildren are going to carry on the business ... to the Conclusion

Beings I am an armer... and seeing your store and ...ision, Network news. My... like too have your Catalo... ...u send me one. I sure ... ...le getting one.

Thanking you.

...h winter at about this time ...d to receiving the L.L. Bean, ...og. This morning I read of ...ther and I was saddened. ...ne were good friends of m... ...ever met him and visited ... ...ly once.

...Bean, Inc. is an American ...honesty, quality and fair p... ...t it will always remain, ...more fitting memorial ? ...I extend my condolences ...members of Mr. Bean's...

Sorry to hear the old man is gone.

I've done business with you folks for over 30 years and only got one bum steer (the first time I washed those "Viyella" stockings I couldn't get them on the cat.)

My deepest sympathy to the L. L. Bean outfit in their great loss. It is a real loss to me, even though it has been a long distance friendship, yet a real one. There is another bond between us besides our love of the Outdoors. That is our close resemblance. We both noticed it the first time we met, nearly fifty years ago. It was so striking as to be uncanny.

I first met Mr. Bean while on my way to climb Mt. Katahdin to get stocked in the things I needed, especially a Guide Shirt and Rain Shirt. Both came in handy as I was caught in a "Cap Storm" with its gale driven snow on the very summit.

Just a word about myself: Connecticu[t] born and bred. Seventh generation of my name in Litchfield. Close to 84, strong and healthy, probably due to a half century of outdoor work. Now re[-]tired , rank of Senior Engineer and Senior Forester in U. S. Service.

Sincerely,

Fred[eric]k C Coo[...]

JUST HEARD OF THE
PASSING OF MR. BEAN. SEEMS HE WAS
QUITE A REMARKABLE PERSON.
WOULD SURE LIKE A CATALOGUE. ALSO A
LIST OF OTHER PUBLICATIONS AVIALABLE
QUOTINGS PRICES ETc.
MANY THANKS.

GENTLEMEN:
PERMIT ME TO EXPRESS MY REGRET
AT THE DEATH OF YOUR DISTINGUISHED
FOUNDER ...
PLEASE ALLOW ME TO EXPRESS A TRIBUTE
TO HIM IN THE ONLY MEANINGFUL WAY I CAN,
A WAY I THINK HE WOULD HAVE UNDERSTOOD
AND APPRECIATED ... BY REQUESTING A
COPY OF THE SPRING CATALOG ...
YOURS SINCERELY,

Family & F_____
We feel
friend — _____
ars of do___
you and _____
will g_____
e.
We have _____
Charles & _____
the new_____
to our _____
Lt. _____

Absender: Mrs. J. Baker
Postleitzahl
(Straße und Hausnummer oder Postf_____

MIT LUFTPOST
PAR AVION

POSTKA_____
DEUTSCHE BUNDESPOST
DEUTSCHE BUNDESPOST 20
ELLWANGEN/JAGST
LORSCH/HESSEN

Dear Sir,
Please send me
a copy of your recent catalogue.
Even here in our little valley we
read of Mr. Beans death. I
always believed everything I
read in his catalogue. He
must have been a fine man.

L. L. Bean Inc.
232 Main Street
04032 Freeport, Maine
U. S. A.
(Straße und Hausnummer oder Postfach)

I am saddened to read in the San Francisco
__onicle of the death of Mr. Bean.
While I had the rare pleasure of meeting him
__y once, I felt that I really knew him well, as a result
__ many years with Beans unusual catalogue.
It was indeed a recommendation, when the descrip-
__e matter beneath an article in the Catalogue stated
__r. Bean uses this". I hope that in future years, you
__l continue this custom, perhaps modifying to read
__r. Bean used this".
On one fishing trip to Pierce Pond in the Thirti__
__ad a guide named Bean, who said he was a relation of
__ Bean. If so, he was one to be proud of-the best I ever
__.
Good luck to this wonderful company, and I may sa__
__titution. I hope success for many years to carry on
the LL tradition.
I have lost touch due to years in Europe and
__ I am settled in California, so send me this years
__logue for old times sake-and who knows I may still
__nd a few pennies with you.

I am saddened to read of
__rica's great outdoorsportsman
__ine life he had! I am just on__
__lions who are indebted to him
__st went fishing with my fathe__
__ard Palmer Mason, Pres. for m__
__Mason & Hamlin Piano & Organ C__
__nceton Me. Township, our famil__
__ the ingenious and intelliger__
__ucts Mr. Bean gave the hunte__
__ermen of the U.S., and the wo__
the future to you all.
Sincerely, Gregory__

all of us who had worked for him. He was the guiding spirit of our company and much loved by all," said Leon. "Our company's appeal to our customers was so much a part of his unique personality, however, that we didn't know if we could survive his passing." To underscore that point, the Bean catalog made no mention of the death of its founder. By March 1967, Carl Bean, L.L.'s son, had been voted in as president of the company. Leon was appointed vice president and treasurer.

As no immediate announcement was made of a successor to L.L., rumors swirled up and down Main Street in Freeport. Bean was going to be bought. Bean was going to relocate. They're closing the retail store.

Carl and Leon were destined to clash over the direction of L.L.Bean. Carl was even more averse to growing and changing the business than his father. Leon, well aware of the competitive challenges posed by Abercrombie & Fitch, Orvis, and numerous other catalogers, understood that the company's viability hung in the balance. If L.L.Bean didn't act quickly to update the way it maintained its mailing lists, processed orders, kept inventory, and accounted for income and expenditures, the company stood to join failed outdoor mail-order competitors like Corcoran's, the Alaska Sleeping Bag Company and Herter's on the trash heap.

The tug-of-war between Carl and Leon was short-lived. Carl, who had been secretly suffering from a terminal illness, died in October 1967, just eight months after L.L. At age thirty-two, Leon was appointed president, a role he would keep for the next thirty-five years. The immediate challenge—and a nice problem to have—was managing the surge of orders triggered by recent adjustments to the catalog offerings. Sales in 1967 spiked 25 percent to $4.8 million and showed no sign of letting up. Two years later, sales had climbed to $7.4 million, a rate of growth that strained Bean's creaking, antiquated infrastructure.

Without L.L. or Carl around to apply the brakes, Leon was finally free to modernize. The pace of change inside the company during the next few years was fast enough to cause the heads of most employees to swivel.

The first major change initiated by Leon was converting the mailing list to computerized operation instead of being hand-typed in 1969. A year later, manufacturing moved out of the Main Street factory/showroom to a bigger, more appropriate facility. Using the vacated space and more square footage that opened up when inventoried products moved into new ware-house space, the retail store was redesigned and enlarged. The company soon purchased a mainframe computer to handle order entry and fulfillment, inventory control, and mailing-list management. A new off-site distribution center

Gorman Heads L. L. Bean Firm

FREEPORT—Leon A. Gorman grandson of the founder of L. L. Bean Inc., was elected president and treasurer of the company at a special meeting of the board of directors held Oct. 18.

He succeeds his uncle, the late L. Carl Bean, who died Oct. 14.

Other officers elected were William E. Griffin, vice president, and Shailer R. Hayes, assistant treasurer.

C. Warren Bean and J. T. Gorham Jr. remain members of the board.

Left: Announcement of Leon's ascendency in the Portland (Maine) *Evening Express.* Opposite: Leon Gorman backpacking in 1985.

THE BEAN CENTURY

Carl Bean, L.L.'s son and company president, dies October 14

Keep it in the family: Leon Gorman voted president on October 18

Four students killed by National Guard at Kent State

First Arab oil embargo

Israeli soldiers wear Maine Hunting Shoes in Golan Heights

1969

1972

1974

1968

1970

1973

Mailing list, 700,000 strong, computerized

Shoemaking departs old Main Street Building for new space

Neil Armstrong walks on the moon

Jonathan Livingston Seagull tops best-seller list

First handheld scientific calculator

Leon nearly stumps judges on *To Tell the Truth* TV show

First bar code scanned on pack of gum

Nixon resigns over Watergate scandal

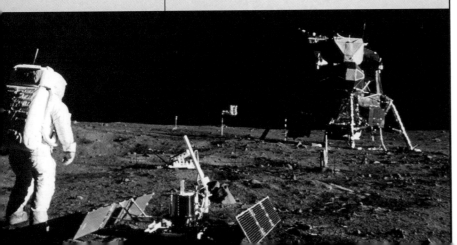

7 73256 62401

Annie Hall wins Best Picture at the fiftieth Academy Awards

Coty Award, fashion's Oscar, goes to Bean. Allagash Hat among stylish items cited

U.S. pulls out of Vietnam

1976

1979

1975

1978

Bean gets its own zip code: 04033

Bicentennial celebrations fizzle

Bean purchases first mainframe computer

Distribution Center expands by 330 percent to keep pace with booming sales

Reactor core damaged at Three Mile Island

Outdoor Discovery School opens

Cover-to-cover color in catalog

L.L.Bean®
Fall 1979

"L.L., you'd hardly know the old store, anymore"

A lot has changed since the old Maine woodsman made his first pair of hunting shoes, but at the same time, a lot of things have stayed the same.

opened in 1974, where new goods were received and warehoused, and orders were filled from the shelves and shipped to customers.

Leon was making good on the Bean promise of putting the customer first, which during the latter decades of L.L.'s life had slipped to become just that, a promise but not necessarily reality. Under Leon's direction, orders were no longer being misplaced. Fewer orders were being delayed for weeks on end because items were out of stock or back-ordered. The length of time from an order being received until it was picked, packed, and shipped out the door shrank. Most important, the company created a Customer Service department, formalizing what had been a haphazard system for handling customer inquiries, suggestions, and complaints. The desire to make L.L.Bean customers happy had always been there, but now it was backed by a disciplined system that would soon secure Bean a reputation for superior customer service not

Above: Leon Gorman took a hands-on approach to managing, scratching off more than four hundred action items as he modernized the company. Left: Leon's influence is discussed in a *Maine Sunday Telegram* article.

just in the mail-order industry, but throughout American business.

One by one, Leon was scratching items from a "to-do" list he had jotted down during the long years when L.L. and Carl were in charge and the status quo ruled. The list, kept in a little black book, had grown past four hundred entries of potential improvements to Bean's operation. One particularly glaring action item remained untouched: the L.L.Bean guarantee. L.L.Bean garnered praise for its guarantee in practically every newspaper or magazine story about the plucky, up-from-the-bootstraps mail-order retailer. The problem was the guarantee hadn't been seen in print since 1919 and wasn't being honored, at least not without a tussle. "Customer returns by mail or in the store were subject to an awkward, time-consuming, and generally unpleasant negotiating contest between the customer and one of our staff," acknowledged

Leon. "Neither party was ever satisfied with the outcome. The procedure didn't make any customer relations sense to me, nor was it economic. It cost us more in haggling time than a full refund or credit at the outset."

A retooled guarantee statement came out in the spring 1968 catalog covering new and unused products. By 1971 the guarantee expanded to cover any product, new or used, for any reason, and was printed in boldface:

> **"Our products are guaranteed to be 100 percent satisfactory. Return anything purchased from us that proves otherwise. We will replace it or refund your money, as you wish, and return your postage costs."**

That unconditional guarantee opened daylight between L.L.Bean and its competition in the outdoors catalog business. Rather than bankrupt the company as some predicted, the guarantee fostered abiding trust and deep

BEST SELLERS, THEN AND NOW

At Bean's fiftieth anniversary, L.L. was still at the helm, and hunting-and fishing-related products dominated. Fifty years later, top sellers have a more everyday slant.

1962

Chamois Cloth Shirt, $5.85

Lounger Boots, $12.25

Warden Jacket, $13.85

Blucher Mocs, $7.90

Ladies' Frontier Pants, $10.85

Maine Guide Shoes, $14.90

Maine Hunting Shoes, $15.85

Chino Pants, $5.40

Hudson Bay Blanket, $30.85

Tattersall Flannel Shirt, $5.90

2012

Men's Double L Jeans, $34.95

Wicked Good Slippers, $59

Bean Boots, $69–$154

Women's Interlock Tee, $12.95–$24.95

Women's Pima Top, $19.50

Men's Double L Chinos, $34.95

Women's Perfect Fit Pants, $39.50

Women's Carefree Unshrinkable Top, $15.95

Men's Premium Double L Polo, $19.95

Men's Oxford Cloth Shirt, $39.95

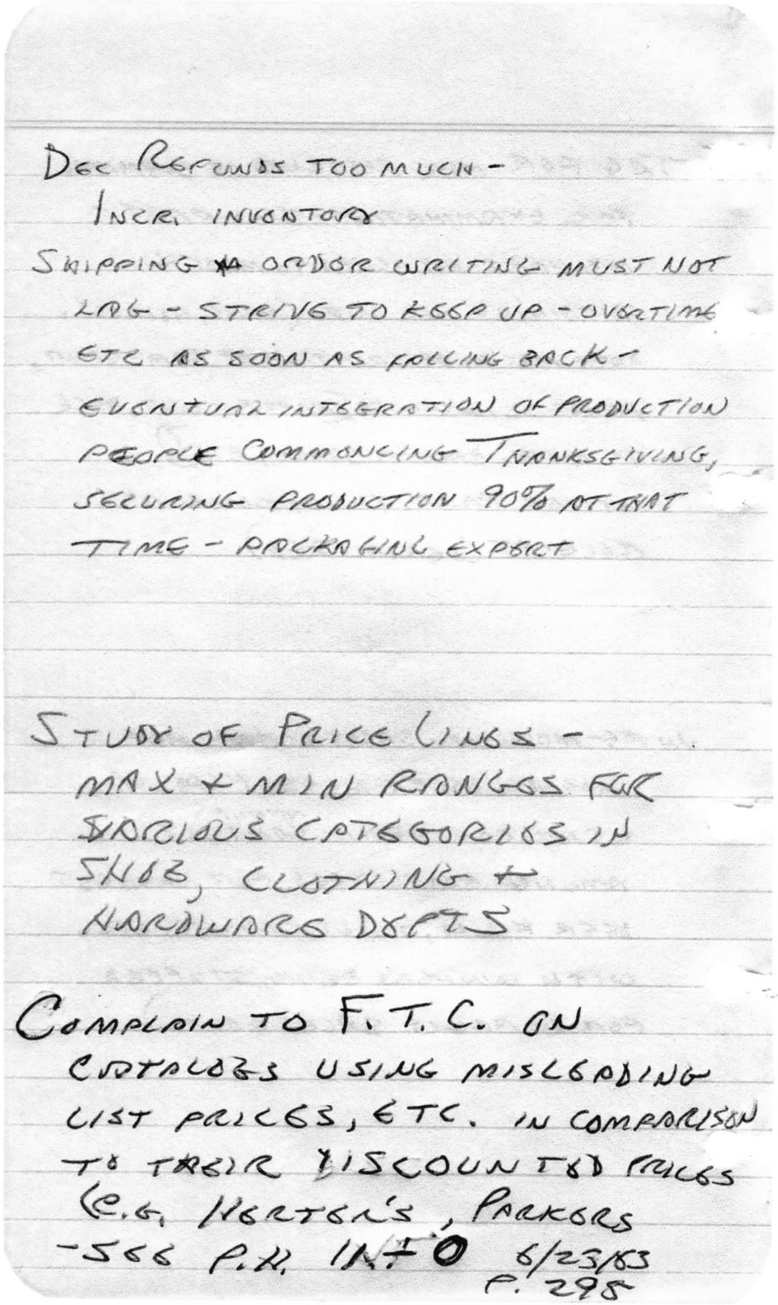

DEC REFUNDS TOO MUCH -
INCR. INVENTORY
SHIPPING & ORDER WRITING MUST NOT
LAG - STRIVE TO KEEP UP - OVERTIME
ETC AS SOON AS FALLING BACK -
EVENTUAL INTEGRATION OF PRODUCTION
PEOPLE COMMENCING THANKSGIVING,
SECURING PRODUCTION 90% AT THAT
TIME - PACKAGING EXPERT

STUDY OF PRICE LINES -
MAX + MIN RANGES FOR
VARIOUS CATEGORIES IN
SHOE, CLOTHING +
HARDWARE DEPTS

COMPLAIN TO F.T.C. ON
CATALOGS USING MISLEADING
LIST PRICES, ETC. IN COMPARISON
TO THEIR DISCOUNTED PRICES
(E.G. HERTER'S, PARKERS
-SEE P.H. INFO 6/25/83
                    P. 295

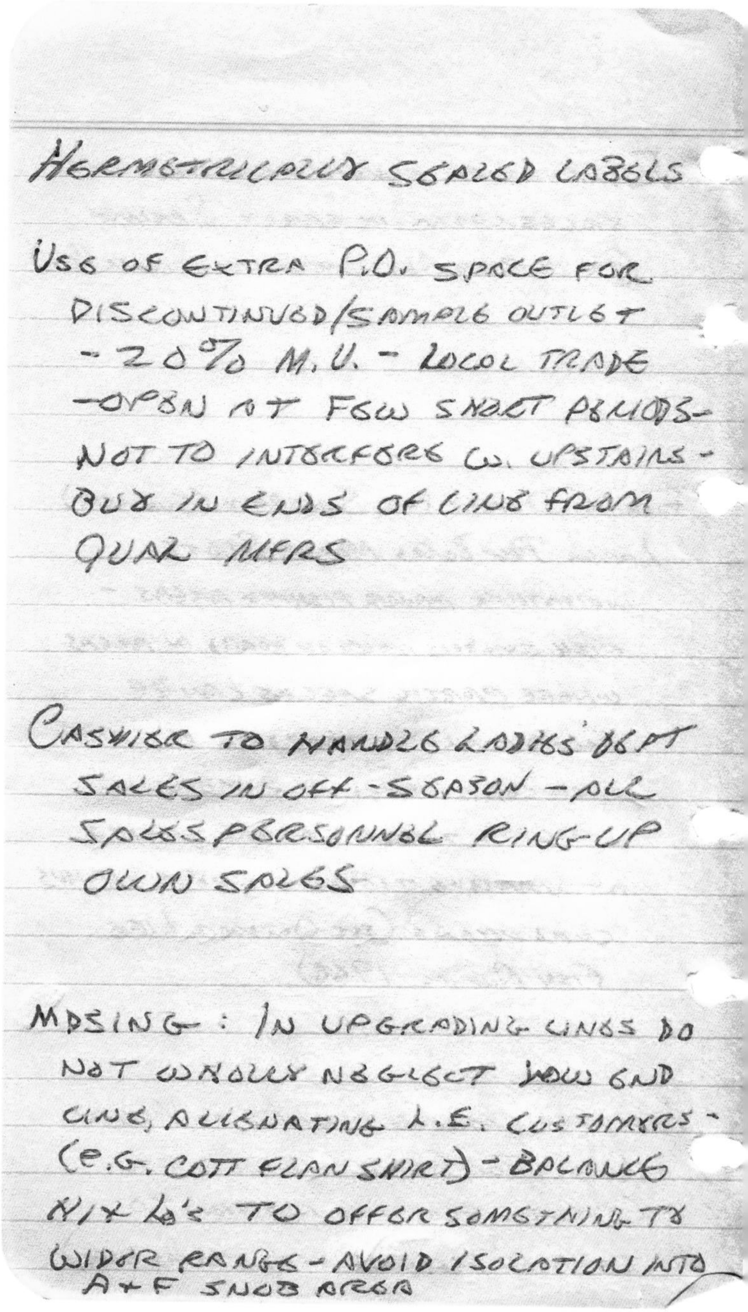

HERMETICALLY SEALED LABELS

USE OF EXTRA P.O. SPACE FOR
DISCONTINUED/SAMPLE OUTLET
- 20% M.U. - LOCAL TRADE
- OPEN AT FEW SHORT PERIODS -
NOT TO INTERFERE W. UPSTAIRS -
BUY IN ENDS OF LINE FROM
QUAL MFRS

CASHIER TO HANDLE LADIES DEPT
SALES IN OFF-SEASON - ALL
SALESPERSONNEL RING-UP
OWN SALES

MDSING: IN UPGRADING LINES DO
NOT WHOLLY NEGLECT LOW END
LINE, ALIENATING L.E. CUSTOMERS -
(E.G. COTT FLAN SHIRT) - BALANCE
MIX LO's TO OFFER SOMETHING TO
WIDER RANGE - AVOID ISOLATION INTO
   A+F SNOB AREA

FOR ORGANIZATION OF PAYROLL
HANDLING SEE P-N's PAYROLL -
DOT MORSTON HAS

MDSE RETURNED
STAMP SHOULD INDICATE
CONDITION OF ITEM
 1/ NEW
 2/ USED
 3/ ETC. - (SOILED, TORN,
 4/ ESTIMATE OF LIABILITY

HANRE PARKER'S MOTORS IN SALESROOM

PAYROLL REPORT
 THIS YR VS LAST YR

STAND-UP DESK FOR OFFICE

PERSONNEL RECRUITMENT FROM
HIGH SCHOOL - VISIT PRINCIPAL
- MAKE ARRANGEMENTS - PART
TIMERS OR FULL TIME AFTER GRAD

TYPING BY PART-TIME WORKERS
AT HOME - FOR MAILING LIST
CONVERSION (SO MUCH $/NAME)

ANNUAL PAYROLL APPRAISAL AND
ADJUSTMENT - G SUPERVISOR OVER INDIVIDUAL
APPRAISALS W. EMPLOYEE
SEE D+B BOOK

PUT ANNUAL BONUS INTO PROFIT
SHARING?

No. OF ITEMS MADE IN YEAR X COST
OF DIR LABOR ALLOCATED VERSUS
ACTUAL LABOR - DIFF = IDLE TIME IF
A PLUS (CHECK ON THIS)

Four note-filled pages from a small black business notebook used by Leon Gorman from 1960 to 1961. Leon jotted down hundreds of ideas for reforming L.L.Bean while Carl and L.L. remained at the head of the business.

A CLASSIC GETS A MAKEOVER

When it debuted in 1934, the canvas-and-leather Zipper Duffle featured a breakthrough device called the "hookless fastener," aka zipper. It represented a big advance over the snap fasteners on its precursor, the Sportsmen's Kit Bag. The Zipper Duffle remained a Bean mainstay until the mid-1990s, when it was replaced by the indestructible, all-nylon Adventure Duffle, which was full of performance upgrades. In 2010, the Zipper Duffle returned ($175), true to its 1934 self, as part of the Signature Collection.

Zipper Duffle	*3 sizes, 1 color.* *$26, small*

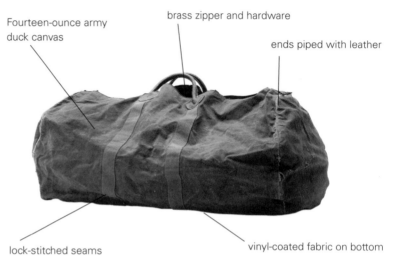

Fourteen-ounce army duck canvas

brass zipper and hardware

ends piped with leather

lock-stitched seams

vinyl-coated fabric on bottom

1½" webbing carrying strap (optional)

Adventure Duffle	*4 sizes, 14 colors. Rolling* *option. $40, medium*

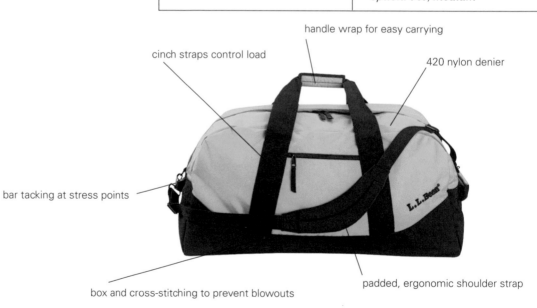

handle wrap for easy carrying

cinch straps control load

420 nylon denier

bar tacking at stress points

padded, ergonomic shoulder strap

box and cross-stitching to prevent blowouts

loyalty. "It became an L.L.Bean hallmark," says Leon. The trick was getting sales staff to buy in. Art Perry, a merchandising manager, was working the floor of the retail store at the time: "Somebody would come through with their family and he'd buy a tent. They'd go to Baxter State Park for a couple of weeks and he'd come back and say, 'The tent leaked,'" remembers Perry. "The poor sales guy would come in off the sales floor and say, 'This guy's stealing us blind.' I'd say, 'I know it. Give him his money back.' And they would, but I'd have to sit guys down…to explain that we'd get it back in the long run. It's a tough concept to get, but it did pay off. But, oh, it just killed the guys."

....

"The world is changing. The old era is ending. The old ways will not do," declared John F. Kennedy with unnerving foresight in his 1960 nomination-acceptance speech. The 1960s, marked by social upheaval and rebellion, would turn every convention on its head. The concept of "business as usual"—even for a business—was about to go from mandate to insult. What nobody could have predicted was how the coming countercultural movements, especially those affecting women's roles, the environment, and the rights of consumers, would create lucrative opportunities for a conservatively run outdoor-apparel and equipment company located up in Maine, far from the centers of the country's unrest.

A whole new breed of outdoor-goer emerged during this era, as people became more inclined to sling a pack over their shoulders than carry a gun or fishing rod. Their interest in the outdoors began out of concern for the environment as well as disdain for urbanization and its associated problems of pollution, overcrowding, and artificiality. Really an offshoot of the back-to-nature movement that compelled young people to abandon cities and suburbs in the late 1960s in favor of organic farms and communes, the boom in backpacking was as idealistic as it was escapist. Nature was more than a destination, the thinking went. It

Above left: The Telephone Order department still operated under a cluttered, analog system in 1970. Above rigth: By 1976, the date of this photo, the Order department was computerized and streamlined.

To Whom It May Concern:

My Mother Karyl Gadecki bought me this backpack around 95'–96' when I was first starting College. That time in my life was incredibly important because everything started to really change and get interesting for me. Little did I know that this backpack would be the catalyst for the next 15 years and last me through: 4 years of college, 1 year with Americorps, 104 mountains, 15 Phish shows, 2 New Countries, 5 ex-girlfriends, 12 new states, 1 cross country move from NY to CA, 14 National parks, 10 years at Stony Picture Television, Countless road trips with best friends and numerous weekend Jam sessions...

It was while writing down this brief obituary of my pack I had realized something. LL Bean doesn't make gear, they make memories.

Thanks for making these memories mine, for I don't know if I could have done it on my own.

Sincerely,

Stephen Gadecki

P.S. After everything that has happened I couldn't just throw my pack out. So I decided to send it back to you, its maker. Please take care of it respectively.

100 YEARS OF GETTING OUTSIDE

BEAN APPAREL AND GEAR GET YOU READY FOR ANY ADVENTURE,
WHETHER YOU'RE HALFWAY AROUND THE WORLD OR
GOING ABOUT YOUR EVERYDAY ROUTINE.

"I am a dog musher and live in northwest Alaska. We go through clothes and gear here like hotcakes. I have two of your anoraks—one for over twelve years—and every day, rain or shine, I have one of them on. You'll notice they aren't clean-looking. Presently, we are competing in local races, including the Kobuk 440, with plans for the Iditarod and the Yukon Quest."

—Tracey Schaeffer, Alaska,
August 4, 2010

"While visiting our son who was studying at the University of Cape Town, my husband and I went to the tip of Africa where the Indian and Atlantic oceans meet. It had been a beautiful day until we got close to the southernmost place in Africa. The currents from the two oceans cause very turbulent waters. It was a good thing we had our L.L.Bean Stowaway Rainwear Parkas on hand. They kept us dry so we could still enjoy this once-in-a-lifetime opportunity!"

—Joan Boehm, South Burlington, Vermont,
January 6, 2004

"Through the decades, L.L.Bean has been my favorite outfitter for outdoor gear and clothing. I am a walking advertisement for L.L.Bean with my hunting vest, hunting coat, fishing vest, jeans, shirts, kayak, snowshoes, hiking boots, running shoes, explorer sandals, travel blazer, watch, hat, etc., and—best of all—four pair of the famous L.L.Bean rubber-bottom boots for all seasons. The gear has kept me comfortable in all conditions. It has been a long winter in Minnesota, but I enjoyed it throughly using my L.L.Bean gear."

—Ed Crozier, Burnsville, Minnesota,
April 18, 2011

Below: Bean's colorful Rainbow Lake Jacket was a 1970s classic.
Right: The famous L.L.Bean Red Felt Hat—well loved and modified by its Connecticut owner, circa late 1960s.

had lessons to teach, principally about humility and connectedness to other living things, for those who were receptive. That was a key point in Colin Fletcher's 1968 *The Complete Walker: The Joys and Techniques of Hiking and Backpacking*, considered the backpacker's bible. That and carrying a stout walking stick. "I go to the wilderness to kick the man-world out of me," stated Fletcher. In a crazy, mixed-up world, nature was the place to find solace and deeper meaning.

Wilderness, the rawest, purest expression of nature, became the grail sought by the legions of new hikers and backpackers. The point was to be alone in the pristine wilds, cut loose from modern convenience. In L.L.'s time, the best hunting was on recently timbered land overgrown with browse for deer. Road access was key for bringing in supplies and carrying out your kill. The backpacking set, known as "nonconsumptive users" to public-land managers, brought only one thing out of the woods: dirty laundry.

An irony about solitude is that when everyone's looking for it, it's hard to find. By 1977, the number of backpackers had grown to twenty-nine million, up from nine million in 1965. "Well into the '60s, a few miles of trail guaranteed peace," wrote Pacific Northwest guidebook author and professed curmudgeon Harvey Manning in *Backpacker* magazine. "Then in the

STYLE OF THE TIMES: 1970s

Now known as the "me decade," the 1970s experienced a spike in people going in search of themselves—and they often headed for the hills (or the mountains, or the shore) to do so. This new breed of outdoor enthusiast— the backpacker—went off the grid seeking enlightenment and the chance to commune with nature, not wild game.

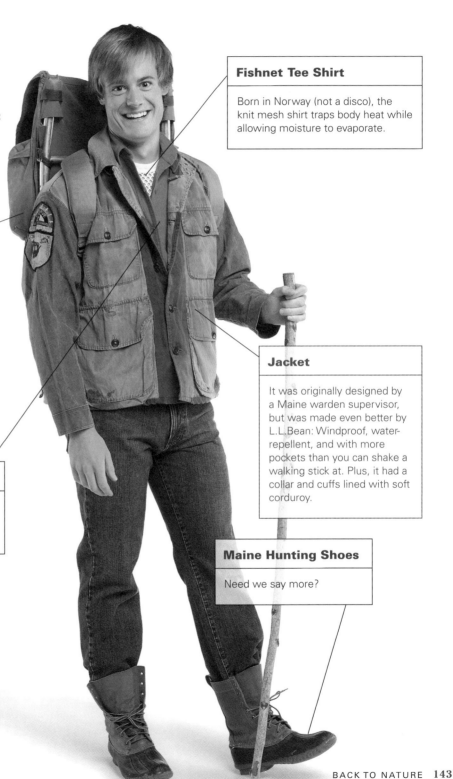

Fishnet Tee Shirt

Born in Norway (not a disco), the knit mesh shirt traps body heat while allowing moisture to evaporate.

Bean's Cruiser Pack Frame and Bag

The aluminum frame makes it featherweight, so it's easy to take off when things get heavy.

Jacket

It was originally designed by a Maine warden supervisor, but was made even better by L.L.Bean: Windproof, water-repellent, and with more pockets than you can shake a walking stick at. Plus, it had a collar and cuffs lined with soft corduroy.

Chamois Shirt

Worn by L.L. himself when he was hunting and fishing. An L.L.Bean classic that gets cozier with each wearing.

Maine Hunting Shoes

Need we say more?

L.L.Bean Staff Model: Lincoln Benedict

Years at Bean: 2
Hobbies: Bike Commuting
Accomplishments: White Mountain Hut Traverse (52 miles, all 8 AMC huts in under 24 hours), 48 4000-footers in New Hampshire
Passions: Ski Touring, hiking, running, movement in general
Favorite Bean Product: Commando Sweater

mid-1960s, just like that, the whole bloody world came apart at the seams! I was horrified to find 300 strangers camped at Cascade Pass, a decade earlier the private realm of my friends and me."

By the mid- and late 1970s, an outdoor-recreation boom was in full swing. All of those backpackers, joined by millions of initiates, were branching out to embrace family camping as well as snowshoeing, cross-country skiing, and canoe tripping, turning once-niche activities into mass markets. Bean was perfectly positioned to meet their expanding needs, for which Leon and his team won praise in the business press. He saw it otherwise. "We happened to be in the right place because we were what we were—real people who enjoyed the outdoors," said Leon. "Our innovation was to do what came naturally in expanding our product lines for people like us."

A curious thing was happening in the outdoors market: a gap was opening between the traditional hunting and fishing audience and the new outdoors people. Though each group was deeply enjoying the outdoors, there were clear demographic differences between them. And while hunting and fishing were still growing, backpacking, bike touring, canoe tripping, cross-country skiing, and the like were growing much faster. The Bean catalog began to reflect those changes. In the spring of 1969, more than one-quarter of the catalog was devoted exclusively to fishing and camping products. Six years later, space for products aimed at this new audience had greatly expanded, and home and camp furnishings such as wood-burning stoves, snowshoe furniture, picnic baskets, cutting blocks, and blankets of every description took up more room than hunting and fishing gear. Although L.L.Bean had always had a large contingent of more casual customers, this was the beginning of a larger vision of who L.L.Bean's customers were, and of a greater intention to serve new audiences without alienating others.

"I'm not sure how L.L. would have reacted

Opposite: Leon leaving for a product-testing trip, 1969.
Right: Hand-tied flies and a lure from L.L.Bean's fishing department in the 1960s.

to the new crowd. But they liked L.L.Bean and, although young, shared the old-fashioned values we stood for," said Leon. "Perhaps this was a reaction to the Vietnam War, or more likely to the environmental movement."

Consistent with their interest in all things natural, the younger outdoor people sought everyday clothing spun from real fibers like 100 percent wool and cotton, rather than cheap polyester and rayon blends. Quality and durability also counted. The consumer movement, begun by Ralph Nader's campaign against the shoddy, dangerous design of American automobiles from Detroit, was influencing every level of the marketplace. No longer content to take whatever products came their way, the buying public demanded value, selection, and performance—all of which played to Bean's strengths.

"We paid close attention to what people were telling us in their letters and in our retail store. In all of our product groups, people wanted lighter weight, longer wear, extra comfort, more safety, higher performance, and easier care and maintenance," recalled Leon. "Item by item we reviewed our product lines and tried to enhance

them with those features that the new outdoors person wanted. We continue today this process of rigorous ongoing reviews of our products and evolutionary improvements whenever appropriate."

Leon, quiet where L.L. had been voluble, methodical where L.L. had been impulsive, had transformed Bean into an organized and efficient operation. The kicked-back, storytelling nature of the company was surely on the wane, but the results were hard to argue with. When Leon took control of the company, he forecast that the company would grow to $50 million in sales by 1980. He was wildly off the mark. Instead, sales reached $121.5 million that year, at a healthy profit margin.

An axiom in the business world holds that doubling the size of a company creates an essentially new company. Bean was now thirty-two times larger than when L.L. was alive. And, unbelievably, the real growth was yet to come. The company's survival after L.L.'s death was long past being in doubt. Now the real question was whether success would spoil L.L.Bean.

Above: Vintage L.L.Bean snow-shoes from 1960. Opposite: The ever-popular Goose Down Vest.

CHAPTER 6

FICKLE FASHION FINDS BEAN

The **NORWEGIAN SWEATER** | First sold in **1965**

FOR A MOMENT IN THE EARLY '80S, FREEPORT JOINED PARIS, LONDON, AND NEW YORK ON THE LIST OF FASHION MECCAS. AS PREPPY STYLE INCREASED IN POPULARITY, CLASSICS LIKE THE NORWEGIAN SWEATER BECAME MUST-HAVES FOR TRENDY YOUNG PEOPLE. BEAN'S FOCUS HAD ALWAYS BEEN ON FUNCTIONAL APPAREL, BUT DEMAND WAS SHIFTING TO CASUALWEAR. RATHER THAN CHOOSING BETWEEN THE TWO, BEAN EMBRACED BOTH, HONORING TRADITION WHILE MOVING INTO THE FUTURE.

Fishing for cod in the North Atlantic is risky business. Always has been. The weather is notoriously foul and the ocean vicious. In the days before survival suits and radio beacons, one slip off the wet, pitching deck of a wooden boat into the cold waters and a fisherman was a goner. In that event, when or if his corpse finally washed ashore, it might be hundreds of miles from home and beyond recognition thanks to the work of crabs and fish. Norwegians, being practical people who had fished these waters for millennia, devised a system that would help identify the deceased and eventually lead to his next of kin being notified. Into the sweaters of the brave men who went to sea they knit distinct colors and patterns, each fishing village with its own. The practice spread to other countries fronting the North Atlantic. In Ireland, the stitching on a fisherman's sweater, not its color, indicated his hometown.

And so it is that the familiar rows of white bird's-eye slashes on the blue background of Bean's Norwegian Sweater mark the wearer—waterlogged or not—as an Islander (pronounced "Ees-lahnder") from Norse settlements on Iceland's east coast. "The pattern is from the oldest sweaters our supplier in Norway has, dating to the 1800s," says Don Rogers, product line manager for men's apparel at Bean. "It's uniquely ours."

The Norwegian Sweater, introduced to the Bean catalog in 1965, was one of Leon Gorman's sly additions that escaped L.L.'s red pencil mark of rejection for all things new and untried. "The sweater met all of the standards of 'Beanness,'" says Leon.

Knit from an 80/20 blend of slightly coarse, unscoured wool and rayon, the original Norwegian Sweater was warm, rugged, and virtually drizzle-and-mist-proof. Unscoured wool is minimally processed to retain water-shedding lanolin and prevent the rough, overlapping scales that surround each wool fiber from flattening and thereby losing some ability to trap warmth.

High-quality materials, combined with a classic style that appeals across generations, makes the Norwegian Sweater not only a perfect family hand-me-down, but also a favorite conversation topic among Bean staffers and customers. Talking about the Norwegian Sweater is something Rogers, for one, loves to do. The sweater, after all, is the reason he's working at L.L.Bean. "Growing up in St. Louis in the '70s, for my tenth birthday my parents gave me the Bean catalog and told me I could pick my gift out of it. I read the description of the Norwegian Sweater, and it sounded like I could trek to the North Pole in that sweater alone.

"I absolutely, positively had to get one. When

Bean's Norwegian Sweater

Long used by Norwegian fishermen who require unusual durability and warmth in a sweater. Heavyweight yarns of 80% unscoured wool for water repellency and 20% rayon for strength. Hand washable in lukewarm suds.

Well proportioned and comfortably fitting for hunting, camping and winter sports.

Color: Navy Blue with White checks.
Men's sizes: Small, Medium, Large and Extra Large.
Price, $12.85 postpaid.

Left: The Norwegian Sweater first appeared in Bean's 1965 Christmas catalog. Opposite: Excited bloggers and Tweeters posted photos and updates all over the web when the Norwegian Sweater reemerged.

Dear L.L. Bean:

Enclosed please find a picture of me and my granddaughter, Lindsay, dressed alike in your sweaters. From the time I saw these sweaters years ago, I wanted one. Somehow, time passed and I never treated myself to one. Then along came Lindsay. She is my miracle girl – having weighed only one pound and three ounces at birth. At my birthday the following year, a friend gave me a coupon to one of the photography shops in our area. And that set off a tradition. Each year right after her birthday, Lindsay and I go to have our pictures taken together. This year, I decided to dress us alike. And, about the same time, your winter catalog arrived, and there were these sweaters, again. And that was all it took. I showed this picture to one of your sales associates at the L.L. Bean store in Columbia Mall, in Columbia, MD and she suggested I send it to you. So here you are. Lindsay is now eight years old and growing taller each time I see her, or so it seems.

Thank you for the many years of receiving your catalog and the nice things I've gotten from your store. This year, especially, thank you! - a dream come true.

Take care and God Bless and Happy Holidays to all of you.

Sincerely,

Leslie and Lindsay Y.
Pasadena, MD

100 YEARS OF LOOKING GOOD

BEAN'S CLASSIC CLOTHING ITEMS, LIKE THE NORWEGIAN SWEATER,
ARE DESIGNED WITH A JOB TO DO: PROTECT THEIR OWNERS FROM THE ELEMENTS,
YEAR AFTER YEAR. THAT NEVER SEEMS TO GO OUT OF FASHION.

"My mother is ninety-four and living in an assisted-living facility. In the process of cleaning out my parents' house we came across the enclosed photo. My father bought this outfit for my mother from L.L.Bean early on in their marriage, in the late 1940s. He was an avid hunter and my mother (on the left) enjoyed the woods but only wore dresses. To this day this is the only pair of pants my mother ever owned!"

—Judith P., Elmira, New York,
November 12, 2008

"In the middle 1980s, I bought from your catalog a felt hat to protect my balding head. Color choices were red and green. I first chose green, but my wife said, 'Get the red one so I can find you at the mall.' Taking her advice, I ordered red.

We lived in Brownwood, Texas, where I was rector of St. John's Episcopal Church. My constant companion was Bruno, a Doberman cross. In the red hat, clad in black, with black Bruno in the backseat of my 1976 green Mercedes diesel, we became local tricolor celebrities.

On my days off, we toured the countryside, visiting isolated 19th-century cemeteries. I read marker and monument inscriptions and planted U.S. flags on graves of veterans of many wars, while Bruno chased jackrabbits, rattlesnakes, and an occasional skunk. At age eighty-six now, I miss Bruno, the country trips, and my old diesel car, but I'm still identified by my L.L.Bean red felt hat."

—The Rev. Radford A.,
Fort Worth, Texas, April 4, 2011

"My highest compliments go to your Norwegian Sweater: a sweater that exceeds the demands of constant punishment from work and weather. The kind of garment we need but find so little of."

—A.P., Nantucket, MA

the Norwegian Sweater finally arrived, I put it on and headed into the woods surrounding our house and hiked the creeks all day. I thought I was the great outdoorsman," says Rogers. "I don't think I took it off until high school." When he had the opportunity to work for the company that made his favorite sweater, he grabbed it.

The same qualities that led Rogers to fall hard for the Norwegian Sweater were meanwhile attracting the attention of students at prep schools and colleges. By the time Lisa Birnbach immortalized it as "the nearest

"*These are Bean's bird-shooting pants, but I never shoot birds, I assure you.*"

thing to a Prep membership card" in her 1980 best seller, *The Official Preppy Handbook*, the Norwegian Sweater was already an old favorite. Sales of the sweater, like everything in the Bean line that was remotely preppy, soared for a few years in the early 1980s before falling back to earth.

Truth be told, the remaining tale of the Norwegian Sweater is not one of continuous produc-

tion according to tried-and-true Bean methods. It's a more complex story of an iconic product that lost its authenticity, slid practically unnoticed into oblivion, and was then revived even better and truer than the original. It begins with a shift in manufacturing from Norway to China in the early 1990s. No more wool from Norway and Scotland, states Rogers; no more ancient knitting tables; no more hand-linking of sweater parts in an old world setting. Half as thick and looking mass-produced, the Norwegian Sweater just wasn't the same, and customers picked up on that. "The sweater lost its magic," admits Rogers.

Sales slipped and slipped—a result of both changing tastes and that loss of "magic"—until the decision to mothball the venerable Norwegian Sweater became inevitable in 1999. Aside from a healthy trade at vintage-clothing shops and on eBay, the Norwegian Sweater was long gone from the market when in 2007, Rogers and the men's-apparel team at Bean picked up on a promising trend. "Americans were putting away their pointy black shoes and putting on work boots," says Rogers. "Bean is not a company that should try to catch the train in fashion trends, but if you're waiting in your station—staying true to Bean's heritage—the train will come back. So we asked, 'Where is that sweater? Could we make that again?'"

The answer was yes. By reconnecting with the sweater's original maker in Norway, the team learned that it could not only reproduce the Norwegian Sweater but do so in 100 percent wool (not the 80/20 blend of the original) without any sacrifice in strength. Advancements in wool spinning meant the Norwegian Sweater also could be lighter and every bit as thick and warm and water-resistant as its predecessor.

Late in 2009 the Norwegian Sweater made it back to the Bean catalog. Traditionalists and the menswear blogosphere were overjoyed. "I'm putting one in my cold-weather arsenal, and chances are it'll be reliably there for years to come," wrote Michael Williams on GQ.com. "I've been waiting for a few months now to get one and just bought a small and medium about five minutes ago on the phone," said a reader of the prep-revival blog Ivy Style. "When L.L.Bean announced the return of the Norwegian, the buzz among menswear blogs was unlike anything I've ever seen.... To say that this sweater is perfect is an understatement. I can't wait to pass it on to my son so he can proudly wear it on campus during the fall season with his green down vest," wrote Skip Brooks on the blog Alex Grant.

The excitement over the sweater's return and escalating sales shouldn't surprise anyone. The sweaters are knit in fjord country, arguably one of the most beautiful places in the world. There's a saying that great milk comes from happy cows: the Norwegan Sweater's quality and resonance are a testament to its origins.

....

For all of the strategic planning and process analysis that go into running a successful company, sometimes plain old luck deals the cards. Such was the case for L.L.Bean when a slim nonfiction title edited and co-written by a brash twenty-one-year-old Manhattanite became a publishing sensation and touched off a fashion frenzy that reached all the way to Freeport.

Lisa Birnbach's *The Official Preppy Handbook*, an insider's satirical but loving take on the rituals and habits of the northeastern upper crust, shot to the top of the *New York Times* best-seller list, a post it would hold for better than a year. When the paper dust settled, the book had sold 2.3 million copies, and L.L.Bean was squarely on the map for those wishing to confirm their membership in old-money circles or fake their way.

Opposite: A drawing by Donald Reilly from a 1982 issue of *The New Yorker*. Above: The original caption for this 1985 *Sports Illustrated* image read, "Bean serves both old hunters and young preppies."

PILGRIMAGE TO **FREEPORT**

BUILD IT—AND EXPAND IT, THEN REBUILD IT, TEAR IT DOWN, BUILD A NEW ONE, DOUBLE THAT IN SIZE, AND THEN DOUBLE IT AGAIN TWO MORE TIMES—AND THEY WILL COME. THE L.L.BEAN RETAIL STORE HAS GROWN FROM ONE SMALL ROOM TO A 175,000-SQUARE-FOOT, STATE-OF-THE-ART RETAIL EMPORIUM COMPLETE WITH INDOOR TROUT POND, ALL THE WHILE BECKONING THE COMMITTED AND THE CURIOUS TO PAY A VISIT.

"It so happens that in 1943 I served as a resident FBI agent in Maine, and my work took me through Freeport almost every day. I met and thoroughly enjoyed the friendship of Mr. L.L. Bean. On one occasion I went there to purchase some hunting boots, having been invited to go on a deer hunt. Mr. Bean would not sell me the boots. He said that he didn't want to sell them knowing I would get to hunt only once, and besides, he confided that the wartime rubber was not worth a damn. He offered to let me use his own boots since we wore the same size, and I accepted.

In July of 1956 on a trip to Canada, I made my parents go 120 miles out of the way so we could visit your store there in Freeport. Since that time, I have continued to receive the catalog and order merchandise from time to time. When I see my parents, I always make a point to show them some article I have ordered through your catalog. It is encouraging to know that a firm like yours exists. Through your dealings with the public it is evident that the guiding principles by which you operate are honesty, integrity, Yankee pride, and initiative. This is saying a lot coming from a born-and-raised Southerner."

—Henry Alton Jones, Jr., October 29, 1971

"Call us Bean Freaks. Our kids are Beanie Babies. We love L.L.Bean and visit your Maine store on our annual trip to Mt. Desert Island/Acadia. We love Maine, and we love L.L.Bean."

—The Kaiser Family, Grosse Pointe Farms, Michigan, January 25, 2006

"About eighteen years ago, I made a trip to Freeport and purchased a pair of black leather shoes, along with other items. Almost a year later, I'd worn the shoes down and took them back up to the store to have the soles replaced. I showed the shoes to the young lady at the Customer Service desk, who walked to a telephone and made a few calls. She came back and told me to go upstairs to the shoe department to get another pair.

I explained that I wasn't looking for a pair of shoes, that I was happy with these. We went back and forth a few times. Finally, I said to her, 'You don't understand. I'm perfectly happy with the way these shoes held up and I'm not here asking for a free pair.' Her response (with a smile): 'You don't understand. While you may be happy with the way the shoes held up, I'm not.' And with that, she turned me into a loyal L.L.Bean customer for life.

—"Shane" (from website), February 22, 2006

"My mother and I lived in Providence, Rhode Island, but had a farm near Waterville, Maine. We would often make spontaneous trips up to 'The Farm.' This was the case one Christmas Eve when I was about nine. 'Let's have Christmas at The Farm!,' my mother declared—the dash was on.

We grabbed presents from under the tree, some cookies for the toll-booth operators, and little else and headed north. Weather-watching was never part of the process. The blizzard hit when we were just outside Portland, Maine, on the 295. A billion light-years from 'The Farm'—but not too far from Freeport. In one of her more inspired moments, my mother with grim determination navigated us through driving sleet and snow to the one place she knew would be open on Christmas Eve, in a blizzard, at what was now the middle of the night—L.L.Bean.

We were welcomed in, given hot cocoa, a PB&J, and our own tent pitched on the floor to ride out the storm in. There were other refugees there that night—apparently we were not the only ones for whom weather watching was not a priority—as well as the people who were working. There were lights and trees and decorations, and everyone was full of cheer.

I fell asleep to the sound of my mother leading the others in a chorus of 'Silent Night.' In a life that has been full of wonder, this is one of my most cherished memories. Thank you, L.L.Bean."

—"Dragongirl" (from website), Fresno, California, March 31, 2011

"In 1975, I was privileged to sail from northern Michigan to Maine. We were on a seventy-two-foot ocean racing yacht. The oldest person on the boat was twenty seven. I was twenty four. I had long hair and wore cut-off jeans, T-shirts, and tennis shoes as normal attire. My hair was down to my waist.

We anchored in Rockland. I left to go home with about forty-five dollars. I hitchhiked back to Michigan but stopped at L.L.Bean because I wanted to visit this legendary place, and I needed a sweater to get back. I found a sweater but also found some cross-country ski slabs on sale. I needed the sweater but wanted the skis.

The sweater was twenty-two dollars. The skis were about twenty. I could not carry the skis, and I would have been broke if I bought both. I asked the clerk if there was anything she could do. She said, 'No problem, we'll ship the skis to you and you can pay for them when they arrive.' Give it up! Long-haired, bedraggled vagabond stops in and she says, 'No problem'? I've been loyal ever since."

—"Born2Run" (from website), Portland, Maine, March 31, 2011

"When I was twelve years old, my family traveled to Acadia National Park during the summer. As we drove north, I remember my father getting very excited at the prospect of visiting L.L.Bean in Freeport. I'd never heard of it and assumed it was either a store specializing in legumes or else something like the department stores I knew in the New York suburbs, with their racks of fancy clothing and a saleswoman spraying perfume at you as you walked in the door.

When we arrived at our destination and went into the store, it wasn't at all like that. I remember, first of all, the fragrance—the smell of woods and leather and the outdoors. The racks were full of clothes I would have liked to have worn for hikes in the woods or just playing in our yard: they were tough but attractive.

I don't remember whether my father bought anything—most likely he did—but I have made up for it in my adult years since then. When I want 'real clothes,' I pick up your catalog."

— "Dancing Rev" (from website), Oberlin, Ohio, April 1, 2011

For the true
Bean devotee,
a Bean Boot tie,
circa 1980.

Featured prominently in Birnbach's guide to the
fundamentals of preppy fashion were such Bean
products as the Blucher Moccasin ("ideal casual
shoes"), Maine Hunting Shoe ("only Bean's
has the true chain-tread outersole"), Gumshoe
("worn when other people would wear rubbers,
and on any informal occasion in dry weather,
too"), Camp Moc ("as comfortable as a bedroom
slipper"), and Norwegian Sweater ("the collar
will stretch out of shape, allowing plenty of room
for layering").

As decoded by Birnbach, preppies dress by
unspoken rules that stress tradition, attention
to detail, practicality, quality, and achieving the
sporting look—which sounds a lot like L.L.Bean.
No surprise then that the company secured the
top spot in *The Handbook*'s "Where to Shop" section. "Bean's is nothing less than Prep Mecca,"
wrote Birnbach. "The showroom is open 24
hours a day, 365 days a year; consequently, a
middle-of-the-night pilgrimage here is one of the
Prep rites of passage."

Preps, once confined to Martha's Vineyard,
Cape Cod, and suburban outposts like Darien,
Connecticut, and Lake Forest, Illinois, were suddenly running free everywhere. *Time* magazine
picked up the trend early on. Said a 1980 article
titled "Here Comes the Preppie Look," "This
summer and fall, the fashion-conscious woman
will be wearing exactly what the fashion-uncon-
scious woman has been wearing for decades. It
is currently labeled the Preppie Look, though the
style has also been known as Ivy League, Town
and Country, Brooks Brothers, or—in England—
County. Mother would approve."

At L.L.Bean, the fad for preppy fashion had an
immediate and pronounced effect. The mailroom
was flooded with orders. The factory couldn't
keep up and even added extra shifts. The year
after *The Handbook* came out was a record year
for the company, with sales up 42 percent. The
next year, 1982, saw another 30 percent increase,

THE PREP CONNECTION

Lisa Birnbach, author of *The Preppy Handbook*, revisits L.L.Bean.

Bean: Which came first: the prep chicken or the Bean egg?

Birnbach: Preppiness, definitely. The original preppy look and ethos came from England—from boot-wearing, tweed-wearing, scarf-wearing, overdrinking English people. Those English people moved to the colonies, of which Maine was not even an original. And the first Mainers, they weren't preps. They were outdoors people who were wearing the boots because they were practical in Maine. So I don't think L.L.Bean started out to be a preppy clothier, no. It started out as an outfitter and supplier for winterwear and sport. And I'm sure it was only because of the durability and the price and the aesthetics of their products that preps decided, "Oh, I'm going to wear this field coat to the market." Or, "I'm going to wear this down vest that was designed for ease of arm movement while hunting to a rave."

Do you think your handbook pushed prep sales in general, including Bean's?

Absolutely. I've been told so. I understand that sales of the Norwegian Sweater, particularly, went through the roof, and the Boat and Tote. The book wasn't about marketing L.L.Bean, of course—I didn't even speak with them when I wrote it—it was about the truth. And the truth was and is: preps like to buy clothing and equipment from L.L.Bean.

Do you think Bean influenced preppy style?

I think L.L.Bean played a giant role. The original appeal of Bean was its well-made, reasonably priced equipment for outdoor adventure, like those ubiquitous Maine Hunting Shoes. And there's something very cool, at least to preppies, about wearing things that have serious intent. It's just more clever of us. It makes us look smarter, and sporting—and that's very important to us. Think about the trench coat, which is such a

mainstay of a prep wardrobe. It has loops for guns, by God. Any piece of clothing is infinitely more interesting to us if it has a history.

You've written that the Norwegian Sweater is "the nearest thing to a prep membership card." Why?

One reason L.L.Bean became a sort of prep station of the cross is that, in 1980, when *The Handbook* was published, there was just one Bean store and no Internet, so wearing clothing from Bean back then conveyed a certain kind of effort you had to make to get it, which made Bean even more attractive. Plus, the Norwegian Sweater is perhaps the most durable article of clothing there is; there's literally no destroying it. And preppies started out being flinty people.

We are having a bit of a prep moment now, wouldn't you say?

What's going on in the world right now isn't a preppy hysteria like it was in the '80s, but we are definitely having a big, long moment. It's due, I think, to the global recession. In a world in which there are so many uncertainties as there are now, these clothes feel time-tested, safe. They're reassuring, like old friends.

And preps like old friends.

We do. We're fond of sameness, consistency. Why fix it if it ain't broken? Which is a perfect segue back to the Norwegian Sweater. I saw that it now comes in different colors, and I have to say, I have mixed feelings about that. I suppose if I ran L.L.Bean, I might experiment with color, but there is something authentic and original and just right about keeping it exactly the way it was.

Spoken like a true prep.

That's my book, after all!

MARRIED AT (AND IN) BEAN

SOME BRIDES DESIRE VERA WANG. THESE BRIDES CHOSE L.L.BEAN.

Weddings are about love and commitment, which sums up the way some brides and grooms feel about L.L.Bean. To the best of anyone's recollection, the Freeport retail store has played host to three wedding ceremonies over the years. The last was on New Year's Eve 1998, with Cheryl Monat, an L.L.Bean employee at the time, presiding.

Monat was showing the groom-to-be around the store when she asked him who would be performing his ceremony. "He looked at me and said, 'Aren't you a notary?' I said I was, and he said, 'Well, you can do it for us,'" recalls Monat. She neglected to tell him theirs would be her first wedding.

The ceremony, staged on the landing right in front of the big moose, went off without a hitch. Monat remembers customers hanging over the railings watching and cheering. "I think all the people there made the young couple very happy—and vice versa," she says.

Alas, the retail store no longer accepts weddings, but that doesn't stop die-hard Bean brides from expressing their devotion. Emily MacCabe, an outdoors educator at the Maine Department of Inland Fisheries and Wildlife, swapped satin pumps for Bean Boots on her big day. "Honestly, what else would anyone I know expect me to wear?" she laughs. MacCabe and her husband, Kris, tied the knot at the Sugarloaf Ski Resort in Carrabassett Valley, Maine, on February 12, 2011. For their first dance—to Rascal Flatts' "Won't Let Go"—the couple wore Bean Boots. "They're very light," raves MacCabe.

Sherry and Larry Vanderlinden of Anchorage, Alaska, were married in Katmai National Park on August 11, 1984; both Vanderlindens and the person officiating wore "Beanies," as Sherry calls them. "They looked great with my wedding dress," she swears. "Plus, they doubled nicely as running shoes when a great brown bear invited himself to the ceremony." Sherry says she still has her Bean Boots and just might wear them again to her fiftieth anniversary: "They last a lifetime, after all."

Jen and Travis Stitt were married on July 4, 2009, at the Hilton Garden Inn in Freeport, then opted to have their wedding pictures shot at the Freeport retail store. "It's just very much a part of the culture in Maine," Jen says.

"We have adorable photos of the two of us in the living room area of the hunting and fishing store, just moments after we said 'I do.' And the photo of us 'in' the fish tank is one of my favorite photos from the wedding day!" says Jen.

"You marry a girl from Maine," she adds, "and you kinda marry L.L.Bean, too."

Above and below: Jen and Travis Stitt opted to shoot their wedding photos at Bean's flagship Freeport store. *Opposite:* Brides, grooms, and wedding parties show off their Bean Boots, Boat and Totes, and shirts.

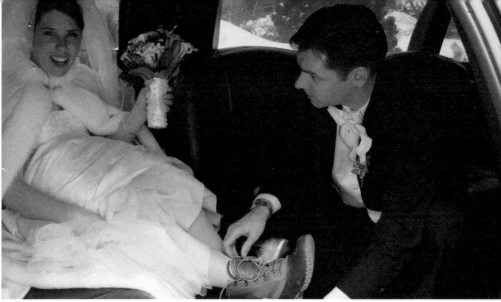

Dear Fine Folks at L.L. Bean...... This photo is just to let you know that way up here in Alaska, at Katmai National Park, Bean Boots are fashionable enough even for a wedding.
This was taken during our wedding ceremony, and if you notice even our marriage commisioner is wearing his " Beanies ".
It was a great ceremony and the Bean Boots not only looked well with my wedding dress, but doubled as running shoes when a great Big Brown Bear envited himself to the ceremony.

In the midst of the preppy boom, a worker selects boxed merchandise from the towering shelves of the L.L.Bean catalog warehouse.

nearly doubling the size of Bean's business in two years.

Everything Bean touched turned to gold. "If we ran an ad, we got more response. If we sent catalogs to a rental mailing list, more people looked at them because they had heard of Bean," said Bill End, Bean's former executive vice president. Even the many knockoffs of its core products, like the Chamois Shirt and Maine Hunting Shoe, boomeranged to benefit the company by raising awareness and sales. The preppy boom had come strong on the heels of the popular outdoor look from the 1970s, which never really went out of style. The company hadn't seen a year like 1981 before, and it wouldn't again. Return on equity, a measure of a privately held company's profitability, hit an astonishing 39.4 percent. "Certainly one of the better performances in retailing history," said Leon Gorman in a speech at the University of Vermont.

As suddenly as the preppy tidal wave swept over Bean, it receded. The wonder is that it lasted as long as it did. After all, a fashion style based on exclusivity can't long endure its own popularity. "So how were the real aristocrats to proclaim themselves? By going punk? Slam-dancing at the Harvard Club?" lamented Lance Morrow in *Time*. "As soon as one finds something to be snobbish about, everyone else has got hold of it…the feeling of being something special vanishes."

By 1983 sales growth at Bean had slowed to 6 percent, healthy by any standard but cause for consternation in some offices at headquarters in Freeport. Leon Gorman, for one, was glad for the slowdown. "Being fashionable was a serious contradiction of our character and brand positioning…. A slowdown would give us time to rethink where we were going," he wrote.

Regardless of whether things had slowed down a bit, L.L.Bean was now a much bigger retailer than it had been a decade before. Topic

STYLE OF THE TIMES: 1980s

When *The Official Preppy Handbook* all but declared Bean the ultimate prep clothier, the products Bean fans had known and loved for decades—the Blucher Moccasin, the Maine Hunting Shoe, the Norwegian Sweater, and others—suddenly became fashionable. "Preppies" popped up nationwide, and it soon seemed as if every man, woman, and child in America owned something from Freeport.

Norwegian Sweater

A cult classic. Almost indestructible, immortalized by *The Official Preppy Handbook,* and revived in 100 percent wool in 2009, to the delight of sartorialists everywhere.

Bean's Bookpacks

One word: ubiquitous. It's quite possible you couldn't physically enter a school without one slung over your shoulder. Accommodated Trapper Keepers and organic chem books alike.

Bean's Puffin Ragg Pullover

Puffins, pine trees, and red flowers! Oh my!

Bar Harbor Corduroy Skirt

Perfect for dropping Skip at the yacht club, attending Junior League meetings, or sipping G and T's on the links!

Bean's Oxford Cloth Shirt

Quality details include a button-down collar, an extra-deep breast pocket, and 100 percent cotton oxford cloth. One never saw it however, as it was always hidden under a Bean crewneck sweater.

L.L.Bean Jeans

Keeping it simple. 100 percent cotton denim. Deep indigo hue.

Maine Hunting Shoe

Rugged enough for the northeastern backwoods... or a driveway in Westchester.

L.L.Bean Staff Model: Kelly Warsky

Years at Bean: 11
Hobbies: Golf, gardening, exercising my sense of humor
Accomplishments: Board of directors, Junior Achievement; commissioner for the Maine Office of Tourism
Favorite Bean Product: The Puffin Sweater...of course!

L.L.Bean Staff Model: Jordan Warsky

Years at Bean: 17
Hobbies: Golf, swimming, soccer
Accomplishments: Part-time '80s model
Hidden Talents: Speed diaper-changing, making the perfect margarita, pool maintenance
Favorite Bean Product: Cresta Hikers

A on Leon's agenda was deciding whether to open retail stores outside of Freeport. One faction inside the company, led by Bill End, argued that the catalog channel was losing its luster. Mailboxes were crammed with too many catalogs and direct-mail letters. Postal rates kept rising. The path to growth lay in expanding retail stores into the mid-Atlantic, New England, and the Pacific Northwest, they said. Leon remained unconvinced. He had witnessed Talbots and Eddie Bauer enter retail and drift away from their catalog strengths. He'd also seen Abercrombie & Fitch attempt cataloging, which hastened that venerable competitor's demise. (The Abercrombie & Fitch that exists now continues the brand name only, which was sold off after bankruptcy.) "Retail did not feel like L.L.Bean. It was a much faster pace, a 'crisis management' style, was more intuitive than deliberative, and was much more promotional," wrote Leon. "Why would L.L.Bean suddenly be able to do what all others had not been able to do?"

A related issue within L.L.Bean—and one brought to the fore by the company's meteoric growth as well as Americans' evolving preference for work and weekend clothing that was less formal—concerned its overall merchandising direction. Since L.L.'s time, the company had made its mark purveying a mix of rugged utility apparel and gear (think Fishing Trousers) and relaxed weekend wear (the Business Man's Shirt). The market had since become more segmented, and the real growth potential, as asserted by some on the management team, was away from products with functional value and toward the stylishly casual. Case in point: the preppy boom. It was time to decide. Which would it be, active or casual?

Leon was sure of one thing: lose the outdoors and you lose L.L.Bean's identity. "The idea of focusing on sportswear and fashiony apparel seemed to me extremely misguided. It would compromise our character and our outdoors positioning and would move away from our fundamental product strengths," he wrote. But Leon was also a realist and recognized that the outdoors market and Bean itself were not the same. The company's size—$237 million in sales in 1983—and the imperative to continue growing dictated product choices. "We needed items with broader appeal and higher volume potential than in the past, and that took us closer to the mainstream trends in the overall retail marketplace," he continued.

Perhaps the biggest wrinkle in the active-versus-casual debate was the changing profile of Bean's customer base. In 1975 one-quarter of customers were women. By 1980 women accounted for fully half of customers. That was before the preppy boom, which brought even more women into the Bean fold.

Women in general were flexing their consumer muscle in the early 1980s. They had entered college and the workplace in earnest a decade before and were now beginning to occupy jobs with higher pay but longer hours. With a hectic work and home schedule to balance, women found catalog shopping suited their lifestyle. It was easy and far more convenient than dashing to the mall in the evening or on weekends. Those gender trends presented great opportunity but were also confounding internal decision-making over the future direction of L.L.Bean. For much of its early history, L.L.Bean was perceived, rightly or wrongly, as a men's brand. Concessions were made to the ladies, but not many. The Maine Hunting Shoe was issued in women's sizes all the way back in 1922, a Ladies' Ski and Hunting Suit debuted in 1935, and Ladies' Dungarees launched in 1950, but anything resembling a full line of women's apparel would have to wait until 1954. That was the year Hazel Bean, wife of Carl Bean, opened a women's showroom in the store. Hazel had some help from L.L.'s wife, Claire,

who convinced her husband that women needed something to do while their husbands shopped for fishing tackle and hunting outerwear.

The female customer was a bit of a mystery to L.L. "Most of them are so style-conscious they like to change their clothes every time they cross the street," he observed. "Naturally, when they're getting outfitted for a hunting or fishing trip, everything must fit just so." L.L.'s first inkling that women might enjoy something other than scaled-down versions of menswear had come a short while before, as recalled by Carlene Griffin, a mainstay who served in a variety of roles over sixty years at the company. "L.L. said to me one day, 'Why don't we have any woman stuff out here?'" she recalled. "I said, 'Because you don't buy any!' He said, 'I guess you're right.

Why don't you see what you can whip up?'"

As the story goes, Griffin dispatched Skip Dyer to Edwards & Walker, a department store in nearby Portland, to get a few pairs of Bermuda shorts. He picked out several hundred pairs of shorts in red and white as well as blue and white—going with a patriotic theme, as it was the Wednesday before Memorial Day. "We found this beat-up old table and the right front leg wobbled back and forth. We put the shorts right up over the head of the stairs," said Griffin. "They can't miss them when they come in. Come Monday morning, we had only two pair left. That was the start of the Ladies' Department!"

In time for the fall 1954 catalog, an abbreviated line of women-specific products was released, including sweaters, boots, socks, shoes, and

Atha Inerson and Hazel Bean out fishing, undated.

THE OFFICIAL PREPPY HANDBOOK

"Look, Muffy, a book for us."

The first guide to *The* Tradition. Mannerisms, Etiquette, Dress Codes, The Family. How to Be Really Top Drawer. *The Legacy of Good Taste, Proper Breeding & the Right Nickname.*

MUMMY   DADDY

The Schools. Boarding vs. Day, Coed vs. Single-Sex, Chapel, Lights-Out, Dining Halls and Study Halls. A Sampling of Mottoes and Memorabilia. The Importance of Getting Kicked Out ....PAGE 69

The Crucial Element. Top-Siders, Loafers, Tassels. *Cuffs a Must.* The Sock Controversy ...PAGE 138

Winning with Ease and Losing with Grace. Lacrosse, Squash, Crew, and Field Hockey. The Sailing Scene. Flotillas, Regattas, Yachts and Yacht Clubs. The Sporting Life. Tally Ho!...PAGE 100

Essays on: THE VIRTUES OF PINK & GREEN REGULATING THE CASH FLOW ORIGINS OF THE PREP SCHOOL THE OLD BOY NETWORK CLUBS AT THE BIG THREE BASIC BODY TYPES

EDITED BY LISA BIRNBACH

THE BEAN CENTURY

***The Official Preppy Handbook* sells 2.3 million copies**

Chris McCormick, future CEO, joins Bean as assistant advertising manager

Items from Our Catalog, a spoof of the L.L.Bean catalog, tops the paperback best-seller list

Motorola cell phone (big as a brick) sells for $4,000

Shotguns go on sale at retail store

Bean rolls out Touring Bicycle ($595), featuring oversize aluminum frames by Cannondale

***The Cosby Show* rules the airwaves**

1981

1984

1980

1983

1985

IBM introduces personal computer

MTV launches

Summer Olympics are held in Los Angeles, California

Maine's delegates to Republican National Convention dressed by Bean, right down to salmon belt buckle

The Bonfire of the Vanities, by Thomas Wolfe, satirizes 1980s excess

Bean turns seventy-five; with revenues of $493 million, the company is number 323 on the Forbes top 400 list of largest private companies

New "sunrise over Katahdin" logo unveiled

Bean wins Cataloger of the Decade award from *Catalog Age* magazine

Berlin Wall falls

Retail store doubles in size again

1986

1988

1990

1980–1990

1987

1989

Space Shuttle Challenger explodes

Leon Gorman's mother, Barbara Bean Gorman, last surviving child of L.L., dies

Maine Warden Jacket, formerly all wool, returns to catalog in all-weather, down-filled form

Leon Gorman and Tom Armstrong climb Mount Everest, part of international "peace climb"

First non-Freeport store, L.L.Bean factory outlet, opens in North Conway, New Hampshire

coats. Hazel Bean would allow none of those functional items in her Ladies' Department in the retail store—particularly the Ladies' Scarlett Underwear. Hazel ran her department like a fiefdom, selling trendy sportswear not otherwise carried in the L.L.Bean catalogs. The success of Hazel's department and that of the first genuine women's catalog offerings left an impression on L.L.: "A man isn't fussy about what he looks like when he goes fishing; he cares about comfort, not appearance. A woman is different. When she goes to the beach, she wants to dress for the beach. When she goes dancing, she wants to be dressed for dancing. When she goes fishing, she wants to be dressed for fishing. There is a great future in this for us and something that the style people will give some attention to if they are smart." L.L. knew an untapped market when he saw one.

Hazel's dominion over product selection in the Ladies' Department would survive the transition in company leadership from L.L. to Leon. By 1975 the Bean catalog offered thirty-four pages of women's apparel, yet few of those products were on display in the retail store. "Hazel was an attractive, stylish lady and liked attractive, stylish clothes," noted Leon. "I used to cringe when I walked through Hazel's department. It was almost 100 percent inconsistent with our outdoors and utilitarian product assortments in the rest of the store."

As much as he wished for harmony between the women's offerings in Bean's catalog and store, Leon had to admit Hazel was onto something. "Hazel's little department in our store did quite well, adding to my frustration. She began selling Fair Isle Shetland sweaters in the early 1970s, and they soon became our most successful women's product, retail or catalog—and a harbinger of things to come," he wrote.

Casual versus active: the old debate within L.L.Bean had deep roots and, in the mid-1980s,

was very much alive, with adherents on both sides. "The company was starting to divide between those who saw Bean as a business and wanted to follow fashion, because that seemed to present the most opportunity for growth, and those who saw Bean as a value system or 'religion' ('bleeding green') and who wanted to stick to the traditional outdoors L.L.Bean," noted Leon. Ultimately, he decided it wasn't an either/or proposition. Active and casual could prosper under the same broad tent. The distinctive Bean take on casual products is that it had to balance function and style.

"Our decision to pursue the two tracks… was based on the idea that our customers were

Opposite: Hazel Bean's Women's Department. Above: Women's Outdoor Specialties Catalog, mid-1980s.

outdoors-oriented people and we were catering to the leisure-time parts of their lives. This was the crucial distinction," said Leon. "Our goal was to serve a particular kind of people, those who valued the outdoors just as we did, and our goal was to sell them the products, active and casual, they need to enjoy their outdoors-oriented lifestyles."

Leon drew the line at "dressy casual," a direction he considered out of character for Bean. In day-to-day practice, finding that line led to an earnest wrangling with product managers that to anyone outside of merchandising would have seemed comical. Oxford shirts in pink, for example, were a hot preppy trend at the time, and their appropriateness for Bean was a big issue. Leon rejected pink, as well as shirts in pinpoint oxford fabric and the whole idea of prominently displaying the L.L.Bean logo on clothing. Chasing fashion trends or trying to get ahead of them isn't Bean's style. Never has been. And that gets back to the company's values, of being grounded in the outdoors, holding a connection to tradition, and selling high-quality apparel that holds up not just physically but also in timeless appeal.

To Leon, the market advantage for L.L.Bean was simple. It came not from being the biggest, most technologically advanced, or lowest-cost retailer. It came from being the best in quality, value, and service. "Keeping things simple was getting more and more complex," he noted.

Left: Coats like this one, modified by its owner on the inside lining, were staples of the early Women's Department. Opposite: Bean's summer 1986 catalog.

L.L.Bean®

Outdoor Sporting Specialties

Summer 1986

CHAPTER 7

TOP OF THE HEAP

The **DELUXE BOOKPACK** | First sold in **1990**

IN THE SPRING OF 1990, CEO LEON GORMAN AND SEVERAL OTHER BEAN EMPLOYEES SCALED THE NORTH FACE OF MOUNT EVEREST, JOINING AN INTERNATIONAL CADRE OF CLIMBERS COMMEMORATING THE TWENTIETH ANNIVERSARY OF EARTH DAY. THE VIEW FROM CAMP III MUST HAVE BEEN INCREDIBLE, BUT EVEN AT 21,300 FEET, LEON COULDN'T HAVE SEEN THE FUTURE. LITTLE DID HE KNOW THAT BEAN'S BUSINESS WAS ABOUT TO VENTURE ONLINE AND INTO RETAIL STORES, AND THAT IN 2001, HE'D STEP DOWN FROM A $1.2 BILLION COMPANY.

Every day brings a new round of torture-testing for a book pack. There's sure to be yanking, dragging, flinging, dropping, kicking, tumbling, sliming, scrunching, and soaking—all while the test subject is stuffed full of sharp-cornered books, pointy pencils, and other school necessities. "Very few other products are used like a book pack: two hundred fifty days a year, eight hours a day, and weekends, too," says Pamela Jones, senior designer for packs and bags at L.L.Bean. "Kids are really tough customers."

A book pack worthy of the L.L.Bean label has to shrug off such abuse year after year, lasting from grade school to grad school. L.L.Bean's first entry into the kids' school-pack market—the Beans Bookpack—broke new ground when it came out in 1982. High-quality, long-lasting book packs sized for children were hard to find. The only real choice a parent had was between flimsy nylon packs destined to disintegrate within one school year and technical rucksacks and leather-bottomed day packs meant for peak bagging and hiking. The rucksacks were certainly tough enough, but their streamlined, teardrop shape and access to the interior through a drawstring opening protected by a hood flap made them inconvenient for kids wrestling with three-ring binders and science projects.

"We were looking at a functional void in the market. The problem we needed to solve was building a pack that's lightweight, durable, water-resistant, and easy to get inside, and fits bulky, square textbooks," says Jones, a twenty-five-year veteran of the company. In the early 1980s, the cutting edge of pack design was advancing rapidly, thanks to new materials and innovative designs, especially in the category of backpacks, those oversize packs used to hold all of the food and equipment needed for a multiday hike in the wilds. New internal-frame backpacks did away with cumbersome aluminum frames through use of sturdy foams. Bean's pack-design team thought it could adapt those break-throughs to build a better book pack.

The building block of the Beans Bookpack (now known as the Original Bookpack) was a new nylon fabric called 420 denier packcloth. On the continuum between super-light para-chute cloth and heavy-duty ballistics cloth, it falls in the middle, a perfect balancing of weight, strength, and abrasion resistance. Coated with urethane, it's nearly waterproof. By heat-cutting all of the pack parts, Bean could prevent the pack cloth from unraveling and fraying. Where the pieces joined, the seams would be bolstered by double-needle stitching. The all-important junction between shoulder straps and pack body—the failure point on most packs—would be reinforced with a "backtack," a process in which an industrial sewing machine reverses direction numerous times. Backtacking is used

Imagery from L.L.Bean's 2011 Bookpack campaign.

3-13-07

Dear L.L.Bean,

I had my bookbag since I was five and now I'm eaight and a half. My mom and dad will only let me get a new one if my bookbag wears out. How do I wear it out? Can you plese tell me?

from,
Ellie Thannings

P.S
Happy Saint Patrick Day.

100 YEARS OF COMPANIONSHIP

FRIENDS SHOULD BE AS CONSTANT AS AN L.L. BEAN BOOKPACK,
FAITHFUL SIDEKICK FROM GRADE SCHOOL TO GRAD SCHOOL AND BEYOND.
CUSTOMERS SURE DO GET ATTACHED.

"A year and a half ago my daughter, son-in-law, and four grandchlidren moved from New Hampshire to Texas. We live in Vermont and are a very close family, so it was a very hard change for everyone to be so far apart. In the fall of last year the two oldest children started school. Grammy and Grampy wanted them to have something special for school, so we bought them new L.L.Bean book packs. They loved them."

—"biker2011" (from website),
Cabot, Vermont, April 2, 2011

"When my son started kindergarten we bought our first L.L.Bean Bookpack, a little red one, the smallest you sold at the time. He used it for a little while, then went to the next size. Four and a half years later, my first daughter used it. Then two years later, my second daughter used it. When they all outgrew it, it went to Mom—that's me. I used it for cross-country skiing for years. It was just the right size for a light lunch and something to drink. My baby grew up and moved away and wanted to borrow the little red book pack. A few years down the road and a new little one comes along, and guess who is using the little red book pack to go to day care? That pack will be thirty-four this September."

—"grandmomkat" (from website),
Pennsauken, New Jersey, April 1, 2011

"Enclosed is a picture of my daughter, Eliza, carrying my L.L.Bean Bookpack on her first day of elementary school. I purchased this backpack sometime in the early 1980s to use while I was in college. I carried this backpack throughout the '80s and the '90s while getting a master's degree. I was still using this book pack in 2002 as my carryall teacher bag when my daughter was ready to begin school. I reluctantly decided to pass it along to her and had her initials monogrammed on it. Now she is in the second grade and it's still going strong. We are guessing that this Bookpack has been used every day for twenty years. I wonder just how much longer it will last? I will contact you if my first grandchild wears it on his/her first day of kindergarten!!!"

—"SallyW" (from website),
September 30, 2004

How tough is it? We're talking back of the bus tough.

L.L.Bean
DIRECT FROM
FREEPORT, MAINE™

Now our best-selling Deluxe Book Pack®
has comfier shoulder straps, a headphone
port, zipper covers and more. The best news?
We didn't change the price.

SCHOOL BUS

EMERGENCY EXIT

in can't-fail applications like rock-climbing harnesses and parachute packs.

The Bean design team next considered access and organization. A common problem with book packs and rucksacks of the 1980s was a lack of small pockets for holding odds and ends like pencils, lunch money, and found treasures. The designers included a generous front pocket with an organizer panel sewn inside to achieve an on-the-go cubby system. Full access to the main compartment and front pocket would come from strong #8 YKK zippers arranged in an inverted U-shape. Finally, reflective material on the front pocket and shoulder straps would ensure the school-age wearer could be seen when walking in the dark.

Since the 1980s, L.L.Bean Bookpacks have had to pass through L.L.Bean's testing labora-

tory. "We physically test the materials going into the pack—the fabric, the zippers—and the prototype," says Dave DaPonte, who heads the lab. "We'll simulate what a kid does with a pack, like drop his wet pack on the floor or carpet. So we'll do a stain test. We test it for abrasion resistance, tearing strength, ripping under force, breaking strength of the seams, and water repellency. We did a 'cold crack' test, where we put the pack material in a freezer box at minus-twenty degrees Fahrenheit with an instrument that folds the fabric repeatedly to make sure it doesn't crack."

The Original Bookpack took some time finding its audience. Sales grew steadily as word of mouth and reviews in the media spread the story of the indestructible book bag. Before long, the pack had millions of fans as devoted to the product as any Bean Boot lover. For many people, the Deluxe and Original Bookpacks will be their first exposure to L.L.Bean. And first impressions are lasting ones. "The Bookpacks are 'ambassador' products," says Pamela Jones.

Indeed, a longtime owner wrote to L.L.Bean, "The year was 1991. An L.L.Bean Bookpack was the 'in' pack to carry, and I had to have one. I had no idea that twenty years later I would still be using it." Another, one of many multigeneration Bookpack owners, said, "I carried this backpack throughout the '80s and the '90s while getting a master's degree. I was still using this book pack in 2002 as my carryall teacher bag when my daughter was ready to begin school. Now she is in the second grade and it's still going strong. We are guessing that this book pack has been used every day for twenty years."

....

Mountains invite metaphor—especially when the mountain is Everest and a chief executive

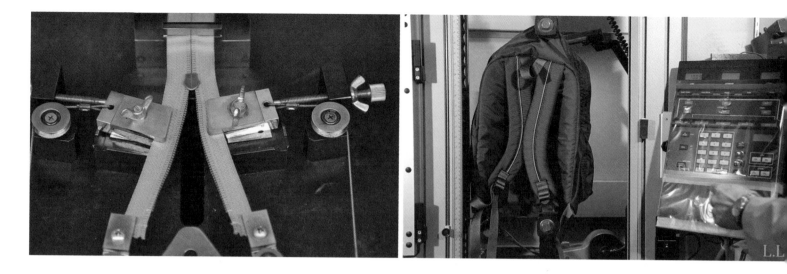

climbs it at a watershed moment in his company's history. In spring 1990 some of the best climbers from the U.S., Russia, and China joined together to scale the north col and ridge of Everest in the name of ecology and superpower cooperation in the wake of the Cold War. The Earth Day 20 International Peace Climb, as it was officially known, was organized by Jim Whittaker, an accomplished mountaineer, the first American to summit Everest, and the former CEO of REI, the Seattle-based outdoor gear and apparel company. Leon Gorman and several other Bean employees would join the expedition high on the world's tallest mountain.

Beyond the obvious goal of gaining the 29,029-foot summit, the climbers on the expedition would also carry down tons of spent oxygen tanks and other trash left behind by previous climbing parties. The themes of the Peace Climb appealed to Leon. He committed L.L.Bean as a major financial sponsor and supplier of the expedition's gear and clothing.

Leon and Whittaker had struck up a friendship through various industry gatherings, and in 1987 Leon joined a Whittaker-led climb to the top of heavily glaciated Mount Rainier in Washington State. "Jim was a man of strong character, great courage, and magnetic personality," said Leon.

Climbing Everest was a different experience in the pre–*Into Thin Air* era. Only one other party was on the mountain during the Peace Climb, as compared with the scores of groups that can turn Base Camp into a circus today. Leon, who was fifty-six at the time, had no intention of going to the summit. He and a group of trekkers ventured as high as Camp III, aka Advance Base Camp, at 21,300 feet, which required traversing the dangerous Rongbuk Glacier. He helped shuttle supplies up and debris down the mountain. In the end, twenty climbers from the team reached the summit, making the expedition one of the most successful to that point. "It seemed a natural fit with L.L.Bean," Leon wrote. "It was outdoors and active, and would illustrate the quality of our products as well as our commitment to a clean environment."

For L.L.Bean, the 1980s closed a period of unprecedented growth and profitability. Total sales roared past $600 million. Leon and the management team had set lofty goals and met them, confronted challenges and survived them with the character and values of the company intact. Entering the 1990s, the outlook was less certain. The nation was sinking into recession, and there were clear signs that retailing—and in particular the catalog mar-

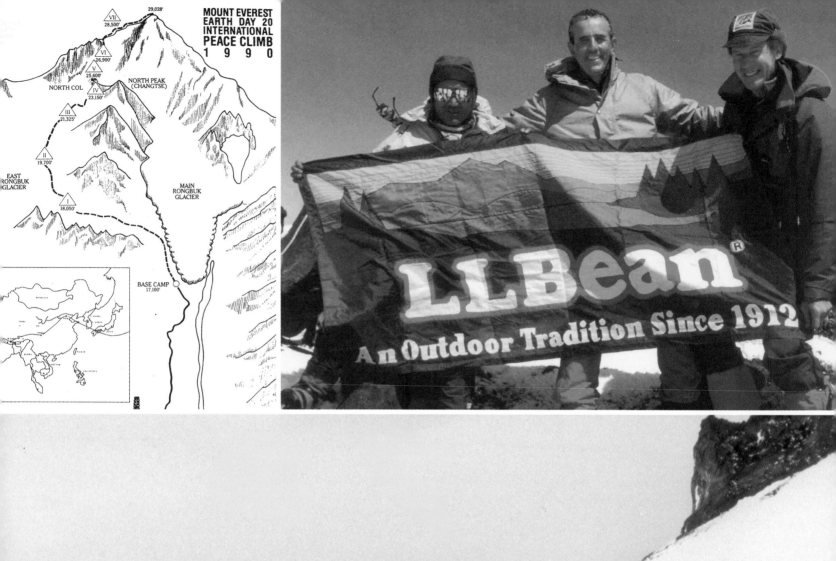

MOUNT EVEREST
EARTH DAY 20
INTERNATIONAL
PEACE CLIMB
1990

VII 28,500'
29,028'
VI 26,900'
V 25,600'
NORTH PEAK
(CHANGTSE)
NORTH COL
IV 23,150'
III 21,325'
II 19,700'
EAST
RONGBUK
GLACIER
MAIN
RONGBUK
GLACIER
I 18,050'
BASE CAMP
17,100'

ON TOP OF THE WORLD

THE BEAN-SPONSORED 1990 PEACE CLIMB PRESENTED THE ULTIMATE FIELD TEST FOR BEAN GEAR AND BEAN EXECS ON MOUNT EVEREST.

There are business trips, and then there's traveling halfway around the world to brave 100-mph winds, crumbling glaciers, and avalanches on the world's tallest mountain. All in the name of work. For L.L.Bean's former president Leon Gorman and current chief merchandising officer Tom Armstrong, the opportunity to participate in the Mount Everest International Peace Climb was too good to pass up.

The climb was to be led by mountaineer and former head of REI Jim Whittaker. "Jim's idea was to take citizen climbers from the three superpowers—the U.S., Soviet Union, and China—and rope up together so our lives depended on one another," says Armstrong. "Let's demonstrate that the superpowers can work together to accomplish great things like global peace and cleaning up the environment." Barely a year removed from the Berlin Wall's coming down and the Tiananmen Square massacre, tensions between the superpowers were running high.

Whittaker, who in 1963 became the first American to summit Everest, would only enlist expedition members who had no prior experience on Everest. "He wanted us all to be equals, five lead climbers and five support climbers from each country," says Armstrong.

Armstrong was selected as a support climber on the strength of his background climbing Mount Denali in Alaska and Yukon's Mount Logan,

Opposite, clockwise from top left: Map of the Peace Climb on Everest; Nawang Gombu Sherpa, Leon Gorman, and Jim Whittaker during a training climb on Mount Rainier; Peace Climb participants.

as well as guiding student climbers in the Teton Mountains of Wyoming. "Our job as support climbers was to haul loads of food, oxygen, and gear up the mountain, set up tents, and just assist the lead guys. Basically, I was a Sherpa," says Tom. Leon met up with the expedition as a trekker. He would eventually climb as high as Advanced Base Camp at 21,300 feet.

"Jim explained to us that international climbing expeditions have a poor track record, because poor communication leads to disagreements and many leave the mountain," says Tom. The Peace Climb, in sending twenty climbers to the summit, ranked among the most successful expeditions to that point or since.

Expedition members were outfitted in off-the-shelf and specially designed L.L.Bean products. PrimaLoft®-insulated Mountainlight Jackets, Polarplus fleece jackets, wind- and waterproof Gore-tex® Everest 90 System parkas and bibs, Cold Weather Boots, and supplex nylon anoraks were just a few of the items team members put through the paces.

"We weren't signaling that Bean was going to get into high-end mountaineering gear, but participating in the expedition allowed us to take a big step up in our outerwear collection. The DNA from those parkas used on Everest carries forward to today's high-end Bean outerwear," says Armstrong.

ket—was simply too crowded. With thousands of new catalogs crammed into mailboxes across the nation, direct marketing was losing luster—and profitability.

The company's prime customer base, the baby boomers, was entering a new life phase. The boomer generation's lust for outdoor recreation had fueled L.L.Bean's spectacular growth, first when they took to backpacking and wilderness canoeing while in their footloose teens and early twenties, then with cross-country skiing, day hiking, and biking as they got serious about careers in their late twenties and early thirties. Now the bulk of boomers were raising families; the leading edge of the generation had even entered early middle age. Whether they would stay in the outdoors or pack it in when confronted by diapers, soccer practices, and creaky knees was an open question.

To youth-obsessed marketers and retailers, boomers were becoming passé anyway. The sporting antics of Generation X, which ran to anything "extreme," were far more compelling. Mountain biking, out-of-bounds snowboarding, ice climbing, bungee jumping—Gen X was undeniably into outdoor pursuits, but only with a shot of adrenaline as a payoff. "No fear" replaced "follow your bliss" as a generational motto. Extreme sports were the rage, but did it make any sense for a venerable outfitter like L.L.Bean to chase an elusive and exclusive niche market?

On top of that, Bean's bread-and-butter niche, rugged utility wear, had gone mainstream. "Everybody—catalogers, department stores, and discounters—was in the rugged outdoors business as well as casual lifestyle apparel. Supply exceeded demand by a lot," recounts Leon. "Retail competition, always intense, intensified. Everybody was getting into each other's channels and product lines."

Hard work and strategic merchandising had brought Leon and L.L.Bean to the pinnacle of their profession, but as Ed Viesturs, a member of the Peace Climb who enjoyed a celebrated career in high places, was fond of saying, "the summit is just a halfway point."

A bright spot in the tough retail environment came from overseas. Japanese consumers had discovered L.L.Bean by the early 1990s. Every day, busloads of Japanese tourists made their pilgrimage to Freeport to shop. Catalog orders streamed in from back home, the Japanese customers willing to wait up to three weeks for delivery of their orders. "Without the slightest attempt on our part to foster growth, we had miraculously developed a substantial and fast-growing customer base in Japan," said Richard Leslie, Bean's international vice president at the time. Anything American was cool with Japan's notoriously trendy youth, and it doesn't get much more American than L.L.Bean.

In Japan, mail order was in its infancy. To reach Japanese customers, for whom presentation, quality, and service were all-important, L.L.Bean needed a bricks-and-mortar presence. Partnering with two large Japanese companies, L.L.Bean opened three retail stores in affluent areas of Tokyo. The first store opened in November 1992 and exceeded forecasted sales by 40 percent. The Bean presence in Japan would peak at twenty-two stores later in the decade. The company had moved decisively and strategically to build market share in the world's second-largest economy, and with it gained invaluable experience in retailing at street level. Sales at L.L.Bean Japan were off the charts, a fact made all the more impressive given that Japan was riding out a prolonged period of economic stagnation during the 1990s known as the "Lost Decade."

In a glowing review of L.L.Bean's Japanese performance in 1996, a magazine writer asked, "With success in Japan by now a virtual lock, a strategic question inevitably arises: Can

"No fear" replaced "follow your bliss" as a generational motto.

THE ART OF **BEAN**

L. L. Bean Inc.
Spring 1944

For generations, the twice-a-year arrival of the Bean catalog signaled that all was still right and good in a fast-changing world. L.L. wrote all of the early catalog copy in a direct, guileless style that fostered what one writer described as "this sense of dealing with an interested and sympathetic neighbor." During the Depression era, L.L. chose uplifting cover art reminiscent of Norman Rockwell. His favorite image was *The Old Country Store,* by artist P.B. Parsons (opposite, top right), which appeared on five different catalog covers and graced the jacket of his autobiography, *My Story.* When Leon took the reins, the company began commissioning original, seasonally appropriate, Maine-based images of hunting and wildlife. Over time, cover themes reflected new ways of enjoying the outdoors and captured Maine's enduring magic.

[About L.L. Bean | What's New | L.L. Bean Products | Park Search | Outdoor Sports]
[Site Index | Contact L.L. Bean | Free Catalogs | Your Opinion? | Credits]

©L.L. Bean, Inc. 1996.
For permissible use, please read this.
L.L. Bean® is a registered trademark of L.L. Bean, Inc.
As such, it may not be used without our permission

The original
L.L.Bean home
page, 1996.

Bean's home run in the Land of the Rising Sun be duplicated elsewhere?" Shortly after those words appeared in print, the Asian financial crisis of 1997 caused the bottom to drop out of a short-lived Japanese economic recovery. The yen plummeted, and Japanese consumers pulled back sharply, especially on purchasing now-expensive foreign goods. By 2000, revenue from Bean's Japanese operations had dwindled to $37 million (from about $210 million at its peak). "The collapse of Japanese sales was one of the most abrupt changes in L.L.Bean's fortunes in my experience with the company," wrote Leon. "We had been riding a wave there and some of us in Freeport thought there would be no end to it."

The seeds of L.L.Bean's long-term growth would come not from Japan or any other country riding a domestic bubble, but from an entirely unanticipated development. Just as Japanese sales crumbled, a retail channel was taking its first steps on something called the World Wide Web. Other alternative media Bean was tracking at the time included the possibility of sending catalogs on CD-ROM or selling by interactive television. The website L.L.Bean unveiled in late 1995 was largely informational, with details about products, the company, and outdoor activities. It was colorful and easy to use, but llbean.com initially only steered customers to the catalog and 800 number. The money-making potential of the web wasn't realized until the next year, when new software allowed Bean (and everyone else) to offer secure credit-card ordering.

The emergence of Internet shopping couldn't have come at a better time. The economics of paper catalogs were getting worse in a hurry. The price of paper was headed through the roof, with the cost of postage right behind. And customers were eager to embrace a fresh, fast way to shop. Traffic and sales on llbean.com grew by leaps and bounds.

At the new millennium, the world of business was gripped with a severe case of dot-com fever. As Wall Street bid up the stock price of speculative start-ups like Pets.com into the stratosphere, L.L.Bean continued building the experience on llbean.com. The medium might have been different, but online shopping proved a natural extension fit for a company that decades earlier had pioneered twenty-four-hour retailing and the convenience of ordering quality products from the comfort of one's home.

By 2000, revenue from llbean.com amounted to 15 percent of total company sales. On November 30, 2010, the website set a single-day record of $2 million in sales—about the same as the company took in for all of 1960. Ten years later it eclipsed catalog sales to become the company's largest income stream.

The web ushered in a decade of change. In business speak, the llbean.com website constituted a "distribution channel" in addition to the

THE BEANEST TOWN IN AMERICA:
LEXINGTON, MASSACHUSETTS

Fans of L.L.Bean—"Beaniacs"—are found everywhere. The company receives orders from every continent and most major cities around the globe. But some places are simply Beanier than others. The L.L.Bean data banks offer ample evidence that people in Maine really love Bean products. No big surprise there. But which town outside that fair state is the Beanest? The number crunchers came back with this answer: Lexington, Massachusetts.

Every household in Lexington (population 30,382) spends an average of sixty dollars on Bean products every year—more than they spend in McLean, Virginia, or Arlington, Massachusetts, two other really big Bean towns "from away." We were impressed. But numbers only tell part of the story.

A suburb of Boston, Lexington is filled with beautiful, well-kept homes, many of which date back to the eighteenth century. The town has a storied history. It is the site of the first shot fired in the American Revolution, in the Battle of Lexington on April 19, 1775, when determined Minutemen

sent British troops scurrying.

"Every time I dropped off my kids at school in Lexington and picked them up, I'd see our backpacks, I'd see our raincoats, I'd see our comfort mocs, and I'd see our Bean Boots. I'd see all our iconic products," says Karen Wright, a longtime resident and, more recently, the manager of customer service at the L.L.Bean store in nearby Burlington, Massachusetts. "Every kid had them. I'm not kidding—every kid."

"I'm not surprised," laughs Mary Hastings, managing director of investments at Wells Fargo Advisors in Lexington, and a notable fan of

Bean in her own right. She thinks she and her two daughters alone might have skewed the results with their purchasing. "Bean is just what we wear. I don't even notice people being especially Beany around town, because it's what I've been accustomed to seeing all my life."

Margery Battin, a longtime Lexington resident and former town moderator for 22 years, agrees: "Everybody here just automatically thinks Bean. And it's not just my generation. My daughter-in-law's stack of L.L.Bean receipts is always quite high."

existing channels of the catalog and the retail stores in Freeport and Japan. In the hyper-competitive, fast-changing retail environment of the late 1990s, this was good, but not good enough. The company needed to open new channels and widen existing ones to stay ahead of the pack.

In rapid succession, the company began a co-branded Visa-card program with banking partner MBNA and a licensing agreement with Subaru to roll out an L.L.Bean Limited Edition Outback wagon for model year 2001. A line of kids' apparel was introduced; the home-products lineup was expanded to include outdoor furniture, games, and gardening accessories, eventually yielding a separate L.L.Bean Home catalog and a dedicated retail store in Freeport; women's apparel was repositioned with more style, color, and sizing

options; and a push to develop new outdoor gear resulted in exciting, critically acclaimed products like Gore-Tex Cresta Hikers, which stand to become the next generation of L.L.Bean icons.

Responding to new business opportunities while staying true to core values—namely enabling lifelong enjoyment in the outdoors—began to pay dividends. Participation in family camping surged as baby boomers took to the woods with their little echo boomers. Visits to national parks rose through the '90s, topping out at 287 million in 1999. Already well positioned in this expanding market with the Bean's Child Carrier, family-size tents, and a wide array of camping gear, the company broadened its offerings. New, high-performing yet inexpensive materials like fleece and waterproof-breathable fabric made it easier than ever to outfit a family in clothing and gear that kept everyone warm, dry, and eager to camp again.

The company took its outdoor mission a giant step further by expanding the Outdoor Discovery School. Beginning in Freeport but today extended to each of L.L.Bean's eighteen retail stores, the Discovery School offers a full slate of hands-on classes in fly-fishing, shooting, biking, sea kayaking, canoeing, and more, all while using Bean products. Customers reserve ahead for half-day and multiday classes or simply walk right out of a store into a quick intro class.

"A walk-on is only ninety minutes long and is mainly focused on introducing people to a sport, having fun, and doing a small amount of instruction. It's designed to help make the sports we support accessible to novices so that they will be inspired to invest in the gear and then take more in-depth classes from us," says ODS manager Gretchen Ostherr.

"There's never been another period when the company did more things—more new things—and it was reasonably successful in most of them," said Leon. "We were building the founda-

tion of L.L.Bean's future."

As the decade came to a close, one last distribution channel remained untested: domestic retail stores beyond Maine. Leon had opposed opening retail stores outside of Freeport since the topic first came up in the early 1980s on the heels of the preppy boom deflating. But the marketplace was changing and, as successful as the catalog had been for almost ninety years, it wasn't telling the fun L.L.Bean story, in part because specialty catalogs for Women, Men, Fishing, Hunting, Kids, Home, and Outdoors segmented the customer base. "Most customers never, ever saw the full range of our outdoors products," said Andy Beahm, assistant treasurer. "Retail stores like our store in Freeport were the solution to that problem… where we can get prospective customers to see L.L.Bean in person and understand the brand and its real outdoors heritage."

The first out-of-Maine retail store in the U.S.—distinct from a factory outlet, the first of which had opened in North Conway, New Hampshire, in 1988—opened in Tysons Corner Center in McLean, Virginia, in July 2000. The suburban Washington, D.C., location is a hotbed for Bean customers and people whose demographics fit the Bean profile. At 75,000 square feet, the Tysons Corner location is considered a "core store" that displays most of Bean's full product assortment amid plenty of wood and stone and natural light. It even has a trout pond. Smaller "discovery" stores soon followed in Columbia, Maryland, and Marlton, New Jersey. With each step into retail, the company learned the ins and outs of staffing, marketing, stocking, and operating stores from a distance. L.L.Bean now operates eighteen retail stores and twelve outlets in ten states.

For all of the ups and downs, competitive pressures, and experimentation of the 1990s, the company still nearly doubled its sales and finished the decade above $1 billion in total

revenue. Leon had an explanation for that: "With consumers' lifestyles becoming busier, reducing the time and inclination for shopping, a highly recognizable store name or brand was essential, especially one that was trusted to provide the product quality and guaranteed service consumers wanted. The L.L.Bean name, backed by our L.L. story and its durable values, continues to be our competitive advantage."

Leon, forward-looking and deliberate in every facet of his role at L.L.Bean's president, began appraising his own career with the same focus in the late 1990s. By his assessment, his role in the company had changed from novice to entrepreneur, then chief merchandiser, manager, and finally strategist. The time had come to find a successor. "The cumulative effect of the stresses and strains was getting to me," he said. "I believed in [L.L.Bean] as much as ever, but I

THE BEAN CENTURY

Nirvana releases *Nevermind*

It's mine: monogramming introduced

U.S. attacks Iraqi forces in Kuwait

L.L.Bean offers first kids' clothing

Bean operators handle 179,112 calls on December 9, a record

Summer Olympics come to Atlanta

1991

1992

1993

1995

1996

Leon Gorman inducted into Direct Marketing Hall of Fame

Bean Boots, cousin of the Maine Hunting Shoe, first appear

First L.L.Bean store opens in Japan

llbean.com launches

O.J. found not guilty

Log on.

www.llbean.com

L.L.Bean

First U.S. retail store outside Freeport, in Tysons Corner, Virginia

Unabomber Ted Kaczynski sentenced to four life terms

1997

1999

2001

1998

2000

Apple releases first iPod

L.L.Bean Limited Edition Subaru Outback introduced

Improvements made to Bean Boot's fit and materials

Napster begins "sharing" downloadable music

L.L. Kids store opens in Freeport

First DVD player hits the market

BEST CUSTOMERS

L.L.BEAN LOVES ALL OF ITS CUSTOMERS; IT'S JUST THAT SOME CUSTOMERS RECIPROCATE MORE. A LOT MORE.

HEIDI McGEE

Visit the rambunctious McGee family at their summer home in Maine or their ski condominium in Vermont, and odds are you'll be sleeping on L.L.Bean sheets, patting yourself dry with L.L.Bean towels, and walking across L.L.Bean rugs. Former attorney Heidi McGee has furnished both homes and clothed three children, top to bottom, in Bean. In the process she's become one of L.L.Bean's all-time best customers.

It all began after she and her husband bought their home in West Boothbay Harbor, Maine. "We're on the water, so we're thinking, 'We gotta have a boat,' so suddenly we've got a Bean kayak. Then we think, 'We can't sit on the porch and look at the boats without binoculars.' So we purchased Bean binoculars. And it snowballed from there."

A Connecticut native, Heidi, forty-five, grew up wearing Bean Boots and carrying Bean backpacks. She occasionally heads to the flagship store when it's raining, but mostly shops online. "I appreciate the fact that if I need to get to a new set of linens, I can do it at five o'clock in the morning from the comfort of my bedroom," says McGee.

McGee's latest purchase was a red backpack for her youngest daughter. "I have a girl, then a boy, then a girl, so I've learned to buy gender-neutral colors, since things from Bean just don't wear out," she says. "Of course, that doesn't mean you can't purchase replacements!"

REVA OLINER

Meet Reva Oliner, sixty-two, a retired school-teacher and housewife from Lawrence, New York, and one of L.L.Bean's top buyers of all time. By her own calculation she has spent "thousands and thousands and thousands" of dollars at L.L.Bean—most of it on duffle bags.

"I'm very blessed with a large social network and extended family," says Oliner, "so I have loads of baby presents and bar and bat mitzvah presents and engagement presents and wedding presents to give." Her go-to gift: the Adventure Duffle, sometimes rolling, sometimes not, but always monogrammed in uppercase block letters.

"I use the L.L.Bean credit card, so I get free monogramming," she says. Whenever Oliner's children and grandchildren gather, they arrive with a candy-hued crush of Oliner's duffles.

"I have this fantasy," she says wryly. "I'm in Miami for Passover along with lots of people from my community, and I'm in the airport, in baggage claim, and I see all these duffles I've given people I love coming down the conveyer belt at once. I see all the initials, all the names. And they're all mine."

wasn't leading it as well as I knew how. It wasn't fair to L.L.Bean to have a president who wasn't fully energized and doing his best every day."

During his thirty-four years at the helm, Leon had grown L.L.Bean from a $4.8 million cataloger with one small retail store into a $1.2 billion brand known worldwide for quality-made products and exceptional customer service. Were L.L. to come back and witness what his grandson has done with the company, he'd be a bit dazzled by its size and complexity, and he certainly wouldn't recognize what has become of his rambling, creaky factory store on Main Street in Freeport. But L.L. would have to be pleased to find his hard-won personal standards still guiding the company.

Two years after it began, the transition process culminated on May 19, 2001, with the board of directors voting to approve Chris McCormick,

general manager of Bean's women's business, as president and chief executive officer. Leon was installed as chairman of the board of directors, the majority of whom were members of the Bean family. Chris became the first nonfamily member to lead L.L.'s company. Starting out in L.L.Bean's advertising department eighteen years before, he had advanced into a senior position in marketing and played a key role in launching Bean's international business, e-commerce channel and credit-card program.

"L.L.Bean customers and the community will continue to see a company with a unique set of values, committed to quality products, excellent customer service, and our outdoor heritage," said Chris on taking office.

The company was still family owned by the Bean family, still sticking to L.L.'s Golden Rule, and still in good hands.

Leon Gorman and Chris McCormick in front of a Bean Boot float decorated for the Bean's Best employee award ceremony, 2001.

24 HOURS *at* L.L.BEAN

BEAN PIONEERED ROUND-THE-CLOCK OPERATION SIXTY-ONE YEARS AGO AND HASN'T STOPPED SINCE.

Bean never sleeps. Late-night travelers and insomniacs know the light is always on at the L.L.Bean retail store in Freeport, open twenty-four hours a day, seven days a week, since 1951. And callers will find a friendly, Maine-accented voice on the other end of the line when they dial 1-800-221-4221 at any hour, day or night. That's the public face of Bean. Behind the scenes is a never-ending swirl of activity that goes into bringing you L.L.Bean quality products. Below is a typical day at Bean.

WEDNESDAY, JUNE 15, 2011

6:05 A.M.

Al Andrews turns the ignition and fires up the diesel engine to his twenty-six-foot Freightliner truck, as he's done every morning since Jimmy Carter was a long-shot candidate for president. With forty-four years of service, Andrews is the longest-tenured employee at L.L.Bean. This morning he's moving three pallets loaded with boxes of overstocked, discontinued, and returned products across Freeport from a mammoth warehouse known as the distribution center to the L.L.Bean outlet store just off Main Street. Customers will purchase an equivalent amount of goods off that store's shelves later today, which means Andrews will be back tomorrow, bright and early, with another load. "My father worked on the sales floor at the retail store for twenty-nine years, and both of my uncles and my aunt worked for the company. I guess I'm a Beaner through and through," says Andrews.

7:15 A.M.

A sheet of bar-coded stickers in hand, Theresa Rogers guides an odd-looking metal cart down an aisle in the "low bay" area of the distribution center on Desert Road in Freeport. Rogers is a picker. Every day, orders from customers arrive at the "DC" in four waves of 30 to 40,000 items. Those orders are out the door in the promised time frame—typically within forty-eight hours—96.7 percent of the time. It's Theresa's and a squadron of other pickers' job to hunt down that women's Waffle Henley, size medium in cranberry, amid the grid of eight-foot-high shelves. She'll slap a "pick sticker" on it—essentially that item's digital license plate—and drop it in the pick carts. Pickers walk up to eight miles a day. Theresa's cart, specially designed by L.L.Bean engineers, looks like a solid metal grocery cart with a short ladder attached at the back so pickers can reach the top shelf. When her cart is full, Rogers wheels it to a docking station above a conveyor belt and pulls a lever; then the bottom of the cart drops away to spill out her pickings.

7:30 A.M.

Many fitness-minded employees arrive at work by bicycle. Bean provides bike racks and places to shower to encourage bicycling to and from work and at lunch hour. On a nice summer day, all forty rack slots are taken, and more bikes lean against the walls. Tom Tero, a copywriter for outdoor equipment, rides twenty-five miles to work from his home in Portland to Freeport, with a stop for coffee in Yarmouth. "That's all I need—a shower and a safe place for my bike," he says. It doesn't hurt that his route takes him along the beautiful Maine coast. L.L.Bean has earned national recognition for being among the healthiest, safest, and best overall work environments in the U.S.

8:15 A.M.

Items ordered by customers and picked from the shelves elsewhere in the distribution center arrive at packing stations one floor below and several lengths of a football field away. It might seem like magic when multiple items ordered by the same customer arrive along with a packing list and shipping label, but it has more to do with a complex choreography of conveyors, bar scanners, and computer tracking. Joan Cyr, a work-flow assistant and a seventeen-year Bean veteran, steps in to help pack during busy periods. It's a point of what she calls "packer pride" to get every order right. On this summer day, some 40,000 orders will ship. During the Christmas rush, outflow jumps to 200,000 boxes and packages daily. Packers, pickers, and other employees at the distribution center spend 3 percent of their workday engaged in stretching exercises designed to avoid repetitive strain injury.

9:40 A.M.

On the Harraseeket River, three miles from Freeport's bustling Main Street, Eric Chase is teaching nine eager students to paddle sea kayaks. Eric is an instructor in L.L.Bean's Outdoor Discovery School, which offers quick, walk-on courses in sea kayaking, canoeing, stand-up paddleboarding, fly-fishing, biking, shooting, and archery in summer, as well as snowshoeing and cross-country skiing in winter. Chase leads the paddlers into calm water, pausing to point out a soaring bald eagle, a curious harbor seal, and a cormorant resting on a dock with its wings spread wide. Three of his students have never been in kayaks before, but in less than two hours they'll know the basics and have a memorable sightseeing experience to boot. "We're from Arizona, where there's not very much water, so we were a little nervous," says Madeline, a first-time kayaker from Mesa, after her Walk-On Adventure. "It was great." Sherri Kaufman and her husband, Dennis, had a different objective in taking the course. "We didn't want to buy kayaks and then find out we didn't like kayaking," she says. "Now we're going to go back to the store and buy a pair."

10:15 A.M.

In Bean's Transportation and Logistics department, director Tim Cahill and his team monitor the supply chain of goods manufactured around the globe and ranging in size from watch batteries to sofas. Far East shipments arrive by container either at the Port of Portland, after navigating the Panama Canal, or by railroad at the international freight-transfer station in Auburn, Maine, after being off-loaded in Vancouver and rolled across Canada. Containers are trucked to Freeport, where they're inspected and off-loaded at the distribution center. T&L is tasked with getting products from Freeport out to L.L.Bean's eighteen retail stores and twelve outlet stores located in ten states. "We get the right product in the right place on time, a movement that can be complicated by labor strikes, natural disasters, or production delays," says Cahill.

10:42 A.M.

A row of seven Critter Lunch Boxes, carefully clamped to Meistergram monogramming machines, receive monogramming simultaneously at warp speed. The exact size, style, and choice of lettering are preset in the Meistergram's computer controls. "The bar code that rides along with the lunch box tells the machine what to do," says Tim Roberts, senior manager of operations. It's the operator's job to squarely position the product that needs monogramming and to double-check the choice of thread color. The Meistergram's single needle makes six hundred stitches per minute and polishes off a monogram in less than three minutes.

11:35 A.M.

With the push of a button, lab technician Jim Couture shoots a shower of pressurized water at a sample of waterproof breathable material that might someday be used in L.L.Bean's line of performance outerwear. If, that is, the fabric passes a battery of tests inside the company's test laboratory, including this rain test. Packed behind the waterproof breathable fabric is a sheet of highly absorbent blotting paper, which Courture weighed before the test. After ten minutes of dousing equivalent to a summer downpour, Courture will weigh the blotting paper again. If it tips the scale at even one gram more from water that's seeped through the high-tech fabric, then that material fails to gain Bean's "waterproof" certification. The test laboratory puts every new fabric, button, zipper, paint, plastic, and other building block through its paces—testing for abrasion resistance, tearing, water repellency, color retention, or cracking in extreme cold—before it can go into an L.L.Bean product. "We try to think of what's going on in the field and relate it to the machines in the lab," says Dave DaPonte, manager of product research and testing.

12:00 P.M.

Lunch hour is health hour at the Bean campus in Freeport, where healthy eating choices are dished out at the Beanery, the company's cafeteria, and a wide range of fitness classes take place. It's all part of Bean's comprehensive Wellness Program, an industry-leading effort to promote maintaining a healthy weight, managing stress, and focusing on heart health. At the Beanery, Healthy Choice entrees are discounted. The company maintains twelve on-site fitness centers, where employees can use machines and free weights, or take part in classes ranging from Yoga, Pilates and Zumba to Nutrition Education, Weight Watchers, Smoking Cessation, and Stress Management. "One of the most frequent comments we receive from employees is appreciation that L.L.Bean cares about them as people," says Wellness Program director Susan Tufts.

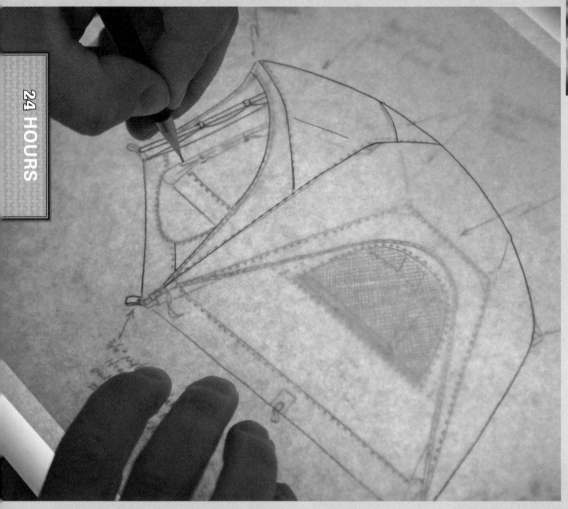

12:45 P.M.

It only looks like Kurt Heisler is playing with a set of aluminum Tinkertoys. He's actually mocking up the frame for a brand-new tent called the Mountain Light 2 XT. Heisler, a senior designer, uses the frame to double-check the dimensions of his concept, which up to this point existed only in a design software program. His product team challenged Heisler to come up with a tent that weighs less than five pounds, is roomy enough for two campers to sit upright comfortably, and is priced below $250. The next step is for Kurt to present his prototype before the tent-and-backpack design group for critique. "'Dry. Simple. Strong.' That's our design philosophy for tents. Any change we make has to improve at least one of those," says Heisler.

1:22 P.M.

Snapped a fly-rod tip or had your watch stop? Chances are Charlene Toussaint will make it right when you return the item to L.L.Bean. Every product sent back to Bean winds up at the Returns department, where front-line employees like Toussaint assess its condition. If the item is still in its original packaging and unopened, it goes back to stock shelves. If it's gently used or like new but discontinued, it goes to one of the outlet stores. If the item has seen some use, it will be sold at bargain prices in the employee store. But if a customer requests his watch be repaired rather than replaced, Toussaint will get it working. She's also a whiz with a sewing machine. She can repair tattered Boat and Totes, frayed Book Packs, Field Coats scissored open by ER docs, and a thirty-year-old flannel nightgown worn through at the elbows. "It's fun to hear from the customer that you did a good job," says Toussaint.

2:05 P.M.

"I love that sunburst." "They all have great expressions. They're having fun in the outdoors." "I don't know, seems like it's about the dog and not the clothes." With each photographic image cast on the big screen inside the pagination room at L.L.Bean's corporate headquarters, comments fly. The team is picking the photo that will grace the cover of the 2011–12 winter kids catalog. Marcia Minter and Susan Berenson lead the group through the slide show of photos taken in late spring at shoots using child models at Breckenridge Ski Resort in Colorado. "This image was shot for inside the catalog, but it's so beautiful I thought I should throw it in for the cover," says Minter of a shot of colorfully clad kids about to launch snowballs at the photographer. The group agrees.

4:40 P.M.

A caller from Danville, Iowa, ordered a pair of wading boots in his usual size, but on arrival they proved too small. He repackaged the boots and sent them back to Bean. Will the replacement pair arrive before his fishing trip this coming weekend? "I'm afraid the boots haven't shown up in our system yet," says Becky Watson. "It could take two and a half weeks. But I'll tell you what. That's our sizing error. I can express-ship a new pair to you so you have them for your trip." Watson, a customer-satisfaction rep, handles every caller with bemused calm. During the off-season around twenty-five reps are on the floor. During the Christmas rush, hundreds more seasonal reps will be brought in. Watson's been solving problems and making customers happy since 1990. "Oh, that won't be necessary. I'll get by," says the caller. "You know, you're much easier to deal with than some other companies, and easier to understand, too." "Thank you," says Watson brightly. "Have a nice day."

5:35 P.M.

One of the best outdoor sports stores in Freeport is as hard to find as a speakeasy. Only a small sign near the door of this converted boot-making factory on a side street betrays the location of the "use room." Inside, racked sea kayaks line one wall; fly rods, cross-country skis, and canoe paddles cluster in special holsters; and shelves are lined with backpacks, sleeping bags, ice axes, snorkel masks, cots, camp chairs, coolers, snowshoes, camouflage hunting apparel, and stoves. And all of it is free to borrow—if you're an employee of L.L.Bean. "It's a nice perk, giving employees an opportunity to get outdoors and use the equipment we sell," says use-room employee Judy Turmenne. Employees borrow through a computerized reservations system. Up to 14,000 items are put to use each year. The most popular? Bike racks and travel luggage.

6:25 P.M.

With a meticulousness usually associated with architects and jewelers, Betty Fuller fusses with a men's winter jacket laid out on a table at Studio 1912 outside Portland, Maine. She's prepping the jacket to be photographed for inclusion in the winter 2011–12 catalog and on the L.L.Bean website. Fuller, a senior photo art director at L.L.Bean, directs a freelance stylist in getting the lighting and look of the jacket just so. "The stylist gives the apparel dimension and shape using tissue paper, Styrofoam, metal pins, tape; there are lots of tricks to the trade," says Fuller. Prepping and photographing the jacket requires forty-five to sixty minutes. Elsewhere inside Studio 1912, L.L.Bean's airy, loft-like studio space, Greg Gorman, also a senior photo art director, supervises a shoot of women's apparel worn by a model flown in from New York City. His team includes a stylist, hair and makeup artist, and photographer. Gorman's model search begins with a review of some two hundred portfolios. "We're looking for someone who is approachable, has great energy, a nice smile—someone our customer can respond to," says Gorman.

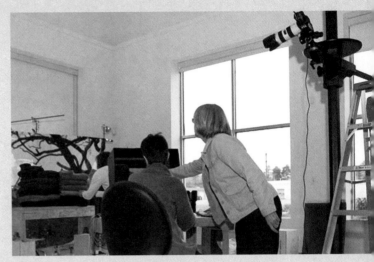

7:45 P.M.

The only thing better than L.L.Bean products is L.L.Bean products marked 30 percent off. That's what brought Lee Farnan to the outlet store in Freeport. Like the other eleven L.L.Bean outlet stores, this one is stocked with an unpredictable array of discontinued, overstocked, and returned products. Closing time is 8:00 p.m., and Farnan is on a mission to find several pairs of pants she can wear to work. She's been a loyal Bean customer for thirty years and couldn't imagine passing up a chance to shop the outlet store while traveling from Altoona, Pennsylvania, with her husband, Bill, to vacation in southern Maine. She hasn't found the right pants yet, but she's clutching a pair of Casco Bay Boat Mocs. "These remind me of when I was a kid," she says. "I might have to buy a little extra."

9:20 P.M.

Outside the crickets are chirping, but inside the bike-assembly room at the L.L.Bean manufacturing plant in Brunswick, Maine, the lights burn brightly, and George Tingfelder and two other technicians are hard at work. Tingfelder is tuning the gears on a women's Acadia Cruiser. Bikes arrive boxed in Brunswick. It's Tingfelder's job to attach the pedals, seat, and handlebars, and then to double-check every component to make sure it's in working order before the bikes are trucked across town to the Bike, Boat & Ski store on Main Street. Each tech will assemble four or five bikes during a workday. Tingfelder likes the quiet of working second shift, which ends at 10:30 p.m., as well as the occasional opportunity to assemble a Felt F3, which retails for $5,100 and is sold only at the Freeport store. "They're nice to work on, like a Rolls-Royce," says Tingfelder.

11:15 P.M.

The Bean Boot and its close cousin, the Maine Hunting Shoe, are its more popular than ever, selling more than a third of a million pairs in 2010. Therefore, the factory where they're made in Brunswick, Maine, throbs with activity late into the night. Charlotte Schleppegrell, who has been with the company twenty-three years, wheels a cart full of V-stays and other boot parts cut from whole cowhide by co-worker Aaron Lee to the skiving area. Skiving machines bevel the edges where boot sections join to create a flat rather than raised seam. "This is my family. We grew up here in the factory," says Schleppegrell. "One reason the Bean Boots are so popular is they're made in the U.S.A., right here. Now we're wanting manufacturing back home. I'm willing to pay a little more for garments to keep jobs here."

THURSDAY, JUNE 16, 2011

12:10 A.M.

It's the dead of night in Freeport, but in Tokyo it's midday. Bill Pond, manager of L.L.Bean's Japanese operations, which include twenty retail stores and Japanese-language web sales, is preparing for a June 30 media event at which creative director Alex Carleton will present the fall 2011 Signature collection to the Japanese press. Pond is also dealing with the aftereffects of the major earthquake that rattled the country. The Japan call center is running off an emergency generator, and the retail store in Sendei is a wreck after dirt and dust shaken loose by the earthquake turned to mud when the sprinkler system went off. "Three aspects of L.L.Bean culture really resonate with the Japanese: love of the outdoors, respect for people, and commitment to quality," says Bill. "Doing things right is very Japanese."

1:05 A.M.

The retail store in Freeport is open for business, just as it has been every night since 1951 with only three exceptions: the night of John F. Kennedy's assassination, the night of L.L.'s death, and when Maine temporarily enacted blue laws against Sunday operation. This early summer night is a quiet one, so sales associate Patty McKeller uses the opportunity to restack men's Double L Jeans. Norm Martineau paints a display wall in the Signature collection area, and David Penley circles by the information counter where free coffee is available for nighttime visitors. Penley has worked the sales floor on the night shift for nine years. "My biggest pleasure is I get to cover the whole store," he says. You never know where a customer will want you next. Tents, boots, hunting and fishing. I get on a family-name basis with customers. They recognize me as much as I recognize them. 'Oh yeah, you helped us last time we were here.' Where else are you going to stop at two in the morning?"

3:20 A.M.

"Hold on, we're going for a ride." With that, the four-ton stock picker, a type of lift cart driven by Paul Maheux, takes off down the central avenue inside the "high bay" storage area at the distribution center in Freeport, then veers sharply left. The machine's onboard computer locks onto a wire guide embedded in the concrete floor, and now he's zooming down a narrow aisle with no more than twelve inches of clearance on either side. "You gotta be comfortable with heights on this job," says Maheux in a vaguely French-inflected accent that gives away his northern Maine roots. He rises fifteen, twenty, then thirty feet off the ground. "Here they are. Fly-fishing rods." Maheux grabs the box, scans its bar code, then drops it on the pallet. Maheux is a trainer who instructs other Bean employees in the use of the lift truck, but tonight he's working on replenishment. As pickers in "low bay" storage deplete boxes during the day by hunting down customer orders, Maheux and the night crew grab more boxes from deep in the "high bay" racks. Those racks rise fifty feet off the floor. During the busiest times of year, as many as sixty lift trucks scramble across the warehouse floor. "Now, let's see how high we can really go."

4:50 A.M.

Dawn's early light brings the first customers. Jim and Audrey Bruderick of Reading, Pennsylvania, left home last night after work and drove straight through on their way to a vacation home two hundred miles farther north in Lubec, Maine. They've stopped at the retail store to buy boots, and David Penley is there to help. "We love it here. We always make our Bean stop when we come through, which we have for twenty-five years," says Audrey. "Coming to Bean is part of the Maine experience. All the people who work here are fantastic, personable, helpful. And you can't beat Bean quality."

5:30 A.M.

L.L.Bean apparel designers shop vintage-clothing stores in the Ralstad section of Stockholm, Sweden. Bean's eighteen designers travel to London, New York, California, and Boston, taking the pulse of the fashion scene. "They're our eyes and ears," says Jim Hauptman, director of design. "Stockholm is a great market for us, because northern Europe is all about function, while southern Europe is about fashion." With the clothing and fabric samples they gather, the design team creates "trend modules" of related apparel back home in Freeport. Several of the influences the team sees for 2012 include work wear, Scandinavian prints, Americana, and Navajo patterns. "Bean doesn't try to be on the cutting edge, but we have to be relevant," says Hauptman. "We'll present these trends in front of the men's and women's teams, giving them inspiration to construct their spring lines. This is where it all starts."

5:45 A.M.

Roe Adams has time to field a few more calls or web chats at the Northport call center before calling it a night. Or a day. Adams has worked as a customer-satisfaction rep for six years. He works at night and is earning his college degree in English by day using L.L.Bean's tuition-reimbursement benefit. After straightening out a shipping situation with a customer in Athens, Greece, via live chat, Adams arranges for a customer in Christiansburg, Virginia, to return a women's Double L Polo in wild berry due to a grease spot. "When I pick up the phone, I know I can make it right," he says. Customer Edmund from Brunswick, Maine, ordered medium but received extra-large. His big bike trip is this weekend. "It's the first-time customer like Edmund I worry about, because he can be a customer for life," says Adams. Adams arranges for the bike shorts to be express-delivered on Saturday morning. Bean will eat the twenty-three-dollar shipping charge. "Sweet!" writes Edmund.

CHAPTER 8

THE NEXT 100 YEARS

The **BEAN BOOT** | First sold in **1912**

IN CELEBRATION OF ITS 2012 CENTENNIAL, L.L.BEAN LAUNCHED THE "MILLION MOMENT MISSION" CAMPAIGN, INVITING CUSTOMERS TO SHARE THEIR FAVORITE OUTDOORS EXPERIENCES VIA SOCIAL MEDIA. WHETHER THOSE WHO LOG ON AND POST STORIES ARE YOUNG NATURE LOVERS OR WEB-SAVVY OLD-TIMERS, IT'S POSSIBLE—IF NOT LIKELY— THAT THEY'LL RECOUNT ADVENTURES INVOLVING THE MAINE HUNTING SHOE. A CENTURY AFTER BEAN'S FOUNDING, THIS SEMINAL PRODUCT REMAINS A FIXTURE IN THE CATALOG—VASTLY IMPROVED AND YET FUNDAMENTALLY UNCHANGED, MUCH LIKE THE COMPANY ITSELF.

In a sequence of practiced motions that takes but forty-five seconds to perform, Brenda Smith re-creates the origin of L.L.Bean—hundreds of times each day. As she first pushes, turns, and then pulls toward her an unfinished boot, her triple-needled Puritan "vamping" machine lays down three neat rows of waxed cotton thread that marry leather top to brown or tan rubber bottom.

Smith's margin for error as she freehands the seam is no greater than an eighth of an inch on either side. So assured is her handiwork that she jokes around with Matt Elwell to her left, who hands her boot halves he has just stuck together after Nora Elwell applied a thin strip of glue to the rubber bottoms. There is economy and precision in Matt's and Nora's movements too. Work like theirs was once plentiful in Maine—shoemaking was the largest source of manufacturing jobs in the state until the industry collapsed in the mid-1980s.

That tradition of Maine leathercraft lives on in the making of the Maine Hunting Shoe and the closely related Bean Boot in Bean's Brunswick factory. It's a commitment L.L.Bean has made to its employees, its customers, and its home state. The notion of making the Maine Hunting Shoe anywhere but Maine is inconceivable. And yet a funny thing happened from doing the right thing: the Maine Hunting Shoe is proving that American manufacturing can be competitive in a global market.

By streamlining the manufacturing process and getting every employee committed to total quality, the factory now makes boots better, faster, and cheaper than ever before. Defects, a big subtraction right off the bottom line, are down 90 percent. Volume is up: the factory will churn out more than 300,000 pairs of Maine Hunting Shoes and Bean Boots in 2011, compared to 219,000 in 1982, at the height of the preppy fashion boom.

It's a long way from the cramped cellar beneath L.L.'s clothing shop, where the Maine Hunting Shoe was first cobbled in 1912, to the light-filled, high-ceilinged manufacturing facility in Brunswick. A high-capacity ventilation system whisks away the faintest whiff of glues and solvents; group stretching sessions on the factory floor every few hours break up the workers' day and help prevent repetitive stress injuries. The boot at the center of all this attention hasn't exactly stood still for one hundred years while the world revolved around it. It's been updated in big ways and small to keep pace with technological advances and remain a step ahead of its many "duck boot" imitators.

The substantive changes to the boot aren't things you see. But stick your feet inside and walk around outdoors on a cold, wet day and you will notice the difference. Which was the point of the boot's most recent retrofit in 1999: retain the boot's outward appearance while overhauling its inner workings. A narrowed heel cup yields a better fit and eliminates the boot's former tendency to suck socks down into a clump; improvements to the arch lend lateral support; the leather upper is softer now and completely waterproof due to a new tanning process; and a new synthetic integrated liner minimizes the buildup of sweat.

Below: L.L.Bean employee Terry Amsden laces a boot. Opposite: Models showcase the Signature collection.

pressure, the bottom is now injection-molded. The old version of the boot bottom was prone to cracking and splitting long before the tread wore out, says Jack Samson. The new bottom is lighter, more slip-resistant, warmer, and substantially more abrasion-resistant, according to the technicians in L.L.Bean's test laboratory.

Owners of the boots, like "Bowlman," a customer from Spokane, Washington, are impressed with the new bottom. "How can you improve a product near perfection already?" he wrote online. "Well, when time came for a resole of a pair of Bean Boots my father got me in the '50s from the original Freeport store, sure enough they really were better!! I'll always be wearing a pair of them."

A major plus in changing boot bottoms was Bean's ability to bring its manufacturing in-house. The vulcanized bottom had been produced in Wisconsin under contract until the late 1990s. Now the thermoplastic soles are made at an L.L.Bean facility in Lewiston, Maine, bringing fourteen jobs to the state.

Style-wise, selection in the Maine Hunting Shoe, which had been straightforward for decades—pick tan or brown, and a height between six and sixteen inches—now has exploded into a wide range of options. Customers can choose from a variety of liners (insulated, shearling, Gore-Tex/Thinsulate) and uppers in full-grain bison leather; colorful quilted nylon (women's only); and navy, green, and blue waxed canvas

A number of the changes to the boot came at customers' suggestion, like stronger laces and the brush guard, a small rim of rubber that nestles up against the leather upper. The guard prevents small sticks from sneaking in between the leather and rubber, which a number of customers had complained about.

By far the biggest performance-related upgrade was to the boot bottom. Previously vulcanized, in a process involving compression-molding rubber onto a form using heat and

Above, left: More from the 2011 Signature collection. Below: Bean boots from through the years.

16 inch   14 inch   12 inch   10 inch   8 inch

Heels 25c. Extra.
Widths, E and F.

Sizes:
Men's, 6 to 12
Boys', 3 to 5
Youths', 8 to 2

OLD BEAN BOOTS NEVER DIE...

THEY GET A NEW LEASE ON LIFE THROUGH L.L.BEAN'S RESOLE SERVICE.

Company founder Leon Leonwood Bean, as flinty a New Englander as they came, saw no reason for tossing away a nicely broken-in pair of Maine Hunting Shoes just because the sole was worn out. "You can have new bottoms put on for about one third the cost of a new pair of boots," he promoted in 1923.

Back then, new soles cost $3.40, or $3.65 with heels. L.L.Bean is still in the business of saving soles on the Bean Boots and Maine Hunting Shoes it sells (it'll cost $39 to $43, depending on whether the boots are lined) and preserving personal histories.

The company rehabs about six thousand Bean Boots and Maine Hunting Shoes a year. The boots pile in at the rate of thirty to forty a day. Some have cracked rubbers (a common issue with the pre-1999 vulcanized bottoms); some have a hole worn through the tread; and

some look like the cat dragged them in. Make that the dog. "We get a lot that have been chewed by dogs," says Scott Ridley.

Ridley works in the repair unit at the L.L.Bean manufacturing facility in Brunswick, the same place new boots are made. Scott first assesses whether the patient can be saved. Some are too far gone. Then he carefully separates the rubber vamp from the leather upper by snipping the three rows of cotton thread. "We get boots that are thirty, forty years old. Had one pair from the 1930s. They went straight to the archives and the owner got a new pair," says Ridley.

The boots next go to Linda Spencer, who has been a Bean employee for twenty-five years. She's the miracle worker who patches torn or rotted leather, retrofits new Thinsulate liners (for an extra charge), and sews together a new rubber bottom with that old leather top.

"Cement workers and dairy farmers are the hardest on their boots," she says. "The chemicals in cement and acids in cow manure eat away the thread."

Every boot upper gets cleaned, conditioned, and polished before it's returned—unless the owner instructs otherwise. "Some people want the battle scars," says Jack Samson, who runs the Brunswick plant. "Or they'll say, 'This is sentimental. Just replace the bottoms.'"

It turns out there is a practical limit to the life span of a Bean Boot or Maine Hunting Shoe: three rebuilds before the leather where it attaches to the rubber bottom becomes so punctured with needle holes that it will no longer hold.

"People are amazed at what we can do," says Ridley. "They send the boots in looking pretty rough, and we send them back looking new. People really get attached to their boots."

To the wonderful folks at LL Bean,

Yes, LL Bean is 95 years old, only a year older than I am. I have just celebrat[ed my]
94th birthday, and have been a loyal customer for at least 45 of those years.

In my days as a professional photographer I travelled the world…wearing my [LL]
Bean pants, long underwear and some very nice shirts. In my off-time I saile[d]
catamarans wearing your foul-weather gear.

Yes, LL's products are great -- and your customer service is truly outstanding[…a]
rarity these days…to find a company that treats me like a friend as well as a v[alued]
customer.

Your patience, your suggestions, your ability to "fix the problem" is unequalle[d]

Thank you for all your kindness…as well as your excellent products.

Dear LL Bean,
Recently I returned a coat and accidentally left my key in the pocket. You guys were kind enoug[h] to mail it back to me. Thank you so much! I appreciate all the eff[ort] made by your wonderful company! Thank you very very much.

I have worn these boo[ts]
Spring, Winter and Seem[?]
turkey hunting, quail, [?]
hrooms, blackberry pic[k]
ral yard and farm wor[k]
They have several hole[s]
m thorns, etc but ar[e]
y servicable and even [?]
nfortable now than w[?]
I am preparing to ord[er]

I have just worn out a pair of your hunting boots after three seasons of service. If any one thinks they have not "gone the pace" and "stood the gaff", they are fully mistaken. I have punished them more in three seasons than most boots get punished in six. I have hunted extensively for more than twenty five years and they are the best equipment I have ever worn.

A "Thank You" to
L.L. Bean Inc.
Freeport Maine
04033

BE RECYCLED. I ALSO HAVE A HOODED PARKA WITH FLYING DUCKS AROUND THE BOTTOM, THAT I CANT GET ANYONE TO WEAR I STILL THINK IT SHOULD BE IN A MUSEUM OF OUTERWARE. IF YOU HAVE READ THIS FAR

Last November, when I was returnin[g] enclosed my checkbook and some cas[h]

As soon as I realized my mistak[e] Department. Not only were they extre[mely] concerned as I was about my loss.

About a week later, I received my chec[k] check made out to me for the cash th[?] thank you enough! Your employees h[?] pass along to them my heartfelt gratitu[de]

Dear L.L Bean,
Thank You for inventing your wonderful products. Your products brought me and my best friend Abby together, on the first day of kindergarten Abby and I had matching L.L Bean backpacks and jackets we thought we were twins so we became best friends.

Thanks Again,

100 YEARS OF MAKING PEOPLE'S DAY

WE LOVE OUR CUSTOMERS, AND FROM THE SOUND OF IT,
THE FEELING IS MUTUAL.

"My dad was in the Pennsylvania National Guard horse cavalry in the early 1930s. They were ordered to maneuvers in North Carolina, which was experiencing a very cold snap.

He wrote my mother to please send him a warm sleeping bag. She ordered one from L.L.Bean. The bag, filled with kapok, was a rectangular canvas with a half tent, designed to protect the upper part of the body. It lived until the later 1960s, keeping me warm as I slept outdoors on our deck here in Colorado, even when it snowed. I've been with you since then."

— RKRB (from website),
Colorado, April 11, 2011

"My brother-in-law was traveling to North Carolina via his Harley motorcycle when it broke down late at night. He was sitting on the edge of the road when a gang of Harley cyclists pulled over, dismounted, and approached him.

He was frightened by the number of them. However, when they got closer, he noticed one of them was wearing an L.L.Bean shirt, so he calmed right down. He decided anyone wearing an L.L.Bean shirt could not be all bad! They came in peace and helped him fix his Harley, and he was back on the road again, with his new friends following to make sure he was all right!"

— "Reney" (from website),
Gorham, Maine, April 1, 2011

"It's a beautifully gusty day in Avoca, County Wicklow, Ireland. I've spent the morning since 5 a.m. tramping the countryside. I drop into Fitzgerald's pub for a bit of lunch. There are only three old men in corduroy sitting at the bar. I'm dressed in Bean jeans, my well-worn Handsewn Mocs, and my equally well-worn Scotch Plaid shirt.

After ordering my lunch, I notice that the old men are giving me the eye. I smile and nod. One says, 'Fine shirt, that.'

'Yes, it's from L.L.Bean,' I say.

The old man scratches his chin and replies, 'I've heard tell of L.L.Bean.'

By the time lunch is over—after I've regaled them with tales of how long-lasting Bean clothes are—all three are headed to the village library to use its computers to check out the Bean website."

— "CapeCodMick" (from website),
Cape Cod, Massachusetts, April 18, 2011

"One summer, when home from college, I was out with some of my high school buddies. We ended up at L.L.Bean around 2:00 a.m. I had worked all day and was tired. I climbed into a tent that was on display and fell asleep. My knuckleheaded friends left me there!

I woke up around 7:00 a.m. I am sure I had been snoring, loudly, but no one bothered me. They just let me sleep it off. I'll always appreciate the night I spent at Beans. One of the nice employees even let me use your phone to call and wake up one of my friends to drive back up and get me. Now that's customer service."

— "Snorer" (from website),
Freeport, Maine, March 31, 2011

"At veterinary school in Ithaca, New York, I experienced the coldest cold I had ever felt. And it lasted for months. Over Christmas break of my first year, while visiting my family, I ordered a warm coat from L.L.Bean. It arrived just as I was leaving for school. I threw it in the car. I arrived in Ithaca during a bitter cold spell and soon realized my new coat was too small. I called L.L.Bean to ask if they had a larger size in stock before I sent mine back, and if they could hold it for me and not sell it before mine was returned."

As I was explaining this to the sales representative, she said, 'Good Lord, child. You can't be in Ithaca without a warm coat. I'm going to ship you that new one today, and you just send that one back when you can.' I received my new coat within about forty-eight hours, long before mine could be returned.

I have never forgotten her kindness, and I have been a faithful L.L.Bean customer ever since! And that mauve winter coat lasted much longer than the color mauve was in style!"

— "Fuzzbuster" (from website),
Connecticut, April 3, 2011

THE RIGHT BOOT, THE RIGHT FIT

Maine Hunting Shoes and Bean Boots aren't your typical footwear. And that goes for fit, too.

Let's clear up any confusion: The Bean Boot is identical to the Maine Hunting Shoe, except its sole is stiffer and longer-wearing. The overall feel is more boot-like. The MHS is more moccasin-like, with a softer, grippier sole that allows the wearer to feel what's underfoot.

When it comes to fit, both boots run larger than most customers are accustomed to. "That's because they're made in America for American feet," says Tom Whitaker, men's-footwear sales representative at the Freeport retail store. Whitaker, who section-hikes the Appalachian Trail in his spare time, has been fitting boots for thirteen years and has this advice on picking the right boot:

Socks. Both boots are sized to be worn with thick socks. Whitaker recommends the heavyweight or midweight merino wool Cresta Hiking Socks.

Miles. If expecting all-day wear covering many miles, go with a snugger fit. Just walking the dog? Looser is OK.

Whole size? Try your regular size first, so if you're a 10, order a 10. Bean Boots and the MHS come only in whole sizes.

Half size? If you're a 10.5, order a 10.

Shearling or Thinsulate liner. The same fitting advice above applies.

Thinsulate plus Gore-Tex. Whitaker says customers report a snugger fit with this liner combo. Order up if a half size, true if whole size.

Rubber Moc. The fit is very generous, says Whitaker. If you're a 10.5, order a 9. If you're an 11, order a 10. "It's made for checking out the garden or the outhouse at camp," says Whitaker.

Height. The three-eyelet gumshoe and six-incher are great for knocking around town or commuting, especially through winter's slush puddles. "The eight-incher will do the job when you're shoveling snow," says Whitaker. The ten-incher is a favorite among college students, worn untied. "The ten- to sixteen-inchers are ideal if you're busting through thick brush in your back forty or portaging a canoe," says Whitaker. "Which height you get is personal preference and depends on how deep the water is you'll be stepping into."

in the L.L.Bean Signature line, which has brought contemporary twists to classic products and revived a number of discontinued items. An all-black version—black bottom and black canvas upper—debuted in autumn 2011. In all, the Brunswick factory makes fifty-six variations on the Bean Boot–Maine Hunting Shoe, according to Samson.

....

Just off Main Street in Freeport, in an addition built onto the back of the white clapboard home Leon Leonwood Bean resided in from 1911 to 1967, L.L.'s life work is kept safe in a walk-in vault. His papers and honoraria fill the many drawers. His memorabilia, as well as select apparel and gear from an illustrious career that spanned half a century, line the shelves. Special racks hold a canoe, oversize sleeping bags, and many, many fly-fishing rods. Being inside the vault is like seeing the pages of the 1936 L.L.Bean catalog spring to life. Special low-UV lighting protects sensitive items from yellowing. A waterless fire-suppression system stands at the ready. The only way in or out is through a heavy metal door that's opened by a security code.

His physical reminders might be hermetically sealed in that archive, but the real spirit of the man who founded L.L.Bean is very much alive in the personal code that guided him as a businessman and outdoorsman. It lies at the heart of what L.L.Bean does to this day. "We have a values-drive culture based upon our belief that our products and our way of doing business truly add significant value to the lives of our customers and all of our stakeholders," says Bean's president, Chris McCormick. "We are not just in any business; we're in a business we are passionate about."

L.L.Bean's practical, timeless clothing continues to find its way into the ensembles of stylish urbanites.

Just one of the many treasures housed at the L.L.Bean archive, this approximately 65-year-old L.L.Bean sweater was formerly owned by Russell Dill of Redlands, California. His mother added the Superman logo.

"L.L.'s Golden Rule reminds us to 'treat people like human beings,' a rule we live by every day," continues Chris. "To do this well and consistently, our workforce is not only committed to the core beliefs and principles but carries them out with honesty, integrity, friendliness, and persistence."

L.L.Bean is rare among corporations in that short-term profit isn't the overriding goal. Being a private, family-owned, family-operated company makes that possible. Without stockholders and Wall Street analysts to answer to, L.L.Bean is not captive to the quarterly results and daily stock-price fluctuations that drive short-term strategy at most public companies. And that won't change going into the company's second century.

Three generations of the Bean family are currently involved in the operation and governance of L.L.Bean, led by Leon Gorman (third generation) as chairman of the board of directors. Bean family members hold a majority of seats on the board (see page 215).

What guides the company is an encompassing stakeholder concept developed by Gorman. Too many public companies, in his view, serve a narrow interest: stockholders only. Bean, on the other hand, believes it has a broader social responsibility.

Translated into the workplace, the concept drives an internal effort to make L.L.Bean a national leader in promoting a safe, healthy, and enriching workplace. "We are always working on some aspect of our environment to make it better," says Bob Peixotto, Bean's chief operations officer. L.L.Bean's salaried employees earn Outdoor Experience days, extra vacation they can partake in as long as it's spent with fellow Beaners and engaged in an activity like hiking, fishing, cross-country skiing, snowshoeing, or biking. To equip themselves for "OEX" days or any weekend adventure, Bean employees head to the use room, really more like a small sports store, to borrow L.L.Bean–branded kayaks, bikes, backpacks, and other products. The whole idea is to encourage everyone to get more engaged with the outdoors and to gain firsthand familiarity with the products the company sells. Then there are the eight cottages the company owns on the shore of beautiful Rangeley Lake, available for daily or weekly rental by any employee and his or her family through a lottery system.

L.L.Bean is proud to have made *Fortune* magazine's list of the "100 Best Companies to Work For," received a C. Everett Koop National Health Award for improving employee health while saving money, and had several of its facilities recognized by the U.S. Labor Department's Occupational and Safety and Health Administration Voluntary Protection Program for making safety and health a top priority.

The stakeholder concept also helps steer L.L.Bean's corporate-giving program, which annually contributes 2.5 percent of the company's pretax earnings toward charitable causes. That compares to a national average of 1 percent for other corporations. "When opening a store in a new community, we engage with conservation and outdoor-recreation interests in the area to find the best way to help," says John Oliver, L.L.Bean's vice president of public affairs. "We contribute funds and volunteers to support key community initiatives." In the Freeport area,

100 YEARS OF FAMILY

THE MORE THINGS CHANGE, THE MORE THEY STAY THE SAME.

Quality. Trust. Service. Those values animated Leon Leonwood Bean and his small store on Main Street a century ago. And they're the same values that drive his grandchildren and great-grandchildren who govern today's $1.6 billion dollar international company.

At its core, L.L.Bean operates under a simple, old-fashioned commitment to doing the right thing. "As a privately held company, we're able to focus on adhering to our values, even if that means the things we do may not be advantageous in the short term," says Shawn Gorman, a fourth generation family member, senior vice president of brand marketing at L.L.Bean and a member of the family governance committee.

Being a private, family-owned business free of Wall Street's quarterly demands goes a long way toward making that possible. Through a family governance committee that reports to the board of directors, members of the extended Bean family connect to the company. "The family governance committee feels it's important to educate the next generation of family members to understand core values. We make sure everyone is actively engaged in governance so we can remain family owned," says Jennifer Wilson, Leon Gorman's daughter and a member of the board of directors and the family governance committee.

The company—and the family— operate under a stakeholder concept. Important business decisions aren't made based solely on the bottom line. The Bean board of directors carefully considers impacts to their communities, their employees, the environment, their family and vendors.

Take as an example the company's efforts to keep jobs in Maine. "It's unusual for a direct marketing company to maintain a distribution center in the northeastern-most part of the country," says Shawn. "But in our family, and in our company, there's a strong commitment to keeping jobs in Maine."

Nate Clark, another fourth generation family director and chair of the family governance committee says, "Our core values—our outdoor heritage, integrity, exceptional service and respect for all our stakeholders—are the rudder that will steer our company into the next century."

Introducing *L.L.Bean*
SIGNATURE

L.L.Bean
100 YEARS

L.L.Bean turns
one hundred

Signature line introduced

Online retail sales eclipse
catalog orders

Business Week names Bean
tops in customer service

Build-your-own
Boat and Tote
introduced

Saddam Hussein
is captured by
the U.S. 4th Infan-
try Division

THE BEAN CENTURY

2002

2004

2009

2011

2002–2012

2003

2005

2010

2012

L.L.Bean "re"introduces
Free Shipping

President Barack
Obama sworn in

Winter Olympics
are held in Salt
Lake City, Utah

President George W.
Bush wins reelection

Facebook is born

Bean has entered partnerships with local school districts to improve education. The company also supports local arts, symphony, and theater. In Maine, Bean is the state's largest corporate donor to the United Way.

Bean also contributes generously toward the conservation and preservation of wild places for people to enjoy in a responsible manner. Here's a sampling of groups and efforts the company supports:

- Since 2002, the company has contributed $3.25 million to Friends of Acadia to support the Island Explorer, a free shuttle service of propane-powered buses that relieves traffic congestion within Acadia National Park.

- The company supports the Student Conservation Association in its efforts to engage youth in restoring national park infrastructure.

- Working through the Trust for Public Land, Bean contributed $1 million to the Katahdin Lake Campaign to assure the purchase of six thousand acres with Baxter State Park to complete Governor Percival P. Baxter's vision of a wilderness preserve.

- L.L.Bean has also been an active supporter of Maine Huts and Trails, helping it build a system of eco-lodges in Maine's western mountains connected by what will be a two-hundred-mile-long trail.

- The Maine Woods Initiative, a land-conservation project in the 100 Mile Wilderness region that supports the local economy through outdoor recreation and sustainable forestry, has benefitted from L.L.Bean's support.

- The Nature Conservancy's St. John River Forest campaign to protect this 130-mile river corridor, one of the nation's premier wilderness canoe routes, is a beneficiary.

Above, top to bottom: Bean employees hike around Costa Rica's Rincon de la Vieja volcano; a directors' trip to Maine Huts and Trails in March 2011; one of the Island Explorer System's thirty ecofriendly buses shuttles passengers around Acadia National Park.

Kids who are exposed to outdoor activities will make outdoor escapes part of their life as they enter adulthood.

Above: An L.L.Bean concert, June 14, 2008.

• To celebrate its one-hundreth anniversary in 2012, the company has launched a campaign called "Million Moment Mission" through social media in which customers recount a favorite outdoor experience. For each experience posted, L.L.Bean will contribute one dollar for youth programming through the National Park Foundation, up to $1 million.

A recent focus for L.L.Bean's corporate-giving program has been getting youth into the outdoors. Young people simply aren't connecting to the natural world as previous generations had. In his groundbreaking book *Last Child in the Woods*, Richard Louv chronicled the temptations and impediments that keep kids from playing outside, from video games to a fearmongering media that stokes parental paranoia about stranger danger to community regulations forbidding backyard basketball hoops and tree houses. "Nature deficit disorder," as Louv calls it, negatively affects kids' creativity, stress levels, and attention span. "We are hardwired genetically to need nature," says Louv. "Playing in nature away from parental surveillance and control gives kids hour after hour of constant energy expenditure, a chance to make mistakes and test their independence."

For an outdoor-recreation company like L.L.Bean, the advent of the indoor child and the attending problem of childhood obesity clouds the future. Kids who are exposed to outdoor activities will make outdoor escapes part of their life as they enter adulthood. "Our challenge, along with others in the outdoor-recreation community, will be to promote outdoor lifestyles to future generations," says Chris McCormick. "That's why a focus of our one-hundreth-anniversary celebration will be on programs designed to get children outdoors and to engage all of our customers in this cause."

Just some of the initiatives L.L.Bean is

STYLE OF THE TIMES: TODAY

L.L.Bean stays true to its founding principles while responding to evolving tastes, materials, and technologies. A flip through the catalog or a trip to Freeport, a satellite store, or llbean.com will lead to many of the tried-and-true products Bean fanatics have loved for decades. But Bean also continues to reflect the changing landscape of customers' lives, with everything from fresh color palettes and cuts to new equipment for outdoor activities on the rise. And of course now, as always, satisfaction is 100 percent guaranteed.

Bean's French Sailor Shirt

First introduced in 1967, this nautical-inspired piece is as *très chic* as ever, equally at home on the coast or in a city café.

Bean's Double L Jeans

Available in four colors, three cuts, and two fabrics; Bean has a jean for every taste and shape.

L.L.Bean Staff Model: Laura M. Serino

Years at Bean: 1
Hobbies: Writing, antiquing, exploring Maine, shopping for vintage clothes
Hidden Talents: "I find and sell vintage clothes online, and I run a fashion blog about Maine. I just can't seem to stop writing about clothes. Oh, and I can play the violin."
Favorite Bean Products: Casco Bay Boat Mocs and French Sailor Shirts

Bean's Handsewn Moccasins

Made of naturally flexible leather that conforms to the shape of your foot, these shoes only get more comfortable over time.

supporting that inspire kids to get outdoors include Healthy Hometowns, a program of the Maine Winter Sports Center to foster youth-centered community outing clubs by providing equipment, counselors, and curriculum in more than four hundred communities in Maine; Take It Outside, a program of Maine Bureau of Parks and Lands that promotes free weekend camping trips at eleven Maine state parks for first-time campers, with equipment donated by L.L.Bean; WinterKids, which provides all Maine middle school students with the opportunity to participate in winter sports activities at recreation areas throughout Maine; and the Appalachian Trail Conservancy, with nearly five hundred thousand dollars in funding to the L.L.Bean Grants to Clubs Program to support hundreds of trail-club projects from Georgia to Maine.

As Leon Gorman always said, business can do noble things.

....

The only way to predict the future is to examine the past. When he started his company based on the strength of a single unique product, L.L. Bean couldn't have known how automobiles, computers, and jet planes would alter American society, much less anticipate the profound dislocations of two world wars, the civil rights movement, and women's entry into the workplace. He would have been hard-pressed to imagine materials like Gore-Tex and nylon, or that his novel idea would grow into a $1.5 billion company that employs more than five thousand people. Yet encoded in the DNA of the company from the beginning were the qualities that would see it prosper through its first century: putting the customer first and making products of the highest quality.

As L.L.Bean enters its second century, the company and the country confront the challenge of an economic downturn unrivaled since the Great Depression. But just as L.L.Bean prospered during the '30s, it's weathering the current economic storm in good stead. Its classic apparel and footwear are selling with renewed vigor, as uneasy consumers seek out durable quality and tried-and-true design. And L.L.Bean Signature's collection of reinterpreted classics drawn from the L.L.Bean archives is connecting with a younger customer swept up in an Americana movement, a revival of so-called heritage clothing brands. In fact, in an article titled "Is L.L.Bean Driving the Runway?" the *Wall Street Journal* put the company at the center of the "Heritage-Hipster Matrix." Compliment accepted, but the company learned long ago not to bank on the fashion world's fickle attentions.

Looking ahead, the only sure thing is that the company will continue to operate by L.L.'s Golden Rule and that people will still seek renewal in the outdoors. "One hundred years from now, our natural environment and the pleasure that comes from escapes to the outdoors will be no less important than they are today," says Chris McCormick. "L.L.Bean will be there to help preserve and protect the precious places to escape, and will be there to inspire and enable successive generations to enjoy their outdoor experiences even as outdoor activities continue to evolve.

"I think L.L. would be proud of what he sees in L.L.Bean today, and of his legacy, built upon by his grandson Leon over his more than half a century of company leadership," continues Chris. "And I would dare venture that, if we do our work well today of instilling our core values in our future company leaders, both L.L. and Leon, while maybe surprised at what they would see in Bean one hundred years from now, would still recognize the foundations they established."

Right: Campaign imagery geared toward the next generation of Beaners.

PHOTO CREDITS

Every attempt has been made to contact the original copyright holders of the materials reproduced herein. Any errors brought to the publisher's attention will be corrected in future editions.

All photographs Courtesy of the L.L.Bean Corporate Collection except as noted.

Collections of Maine Historical Society. Courtesy of Maine Memory Network, online at www. MaineMemory.net: 21 (street); 33; 35 (canoe, dock); 59 (official information); 99 (ice workers).

Studio 1912: 2–3; 6; 8 (bat); 18; 19 (coat); 22–23; 24 (sole); 25 (hats); 30–31 (boot); 30–31 (package); 36 (waterproof dressing); 38; 43 (shirts); 47 (tin cup); 50 (blanket); 53 (decoy); 62–63 (basket); 66; 71 (fish cutout); 72; 74; 78; 84–85 (boots); 86 (knives); 96; 188; 122; 138; 142; 145–146; 148; 158; 163; 170; 172; 188; 204; 208 (boots); 214; 221.

5: Mimi Cotter; 8 (wagon): Courtesy of the personal collection of Jim and Maureen Gorman; 26–27 (assembly photos): Courtesy of L.L.Bean; 30–31 (prohibition): Courtesy of the Library of Congress, Prints & Photographs Division, (plane): Photo by Underwood and Underwood/Time & Life Pictures/Getty Images; 32: Courtesy of the Library of Congress, Prints & Photographs Division; 35 (hiker, kayakers, skiing): by Tom Rafalovich; 40: Photofest; 43 (article 2); The Brunswick Record, 1934; 57 (slippers ad): Courtesy of L.L.Bean, (pet cuddler ad): Courtesy of L.L.Bean; 58 (back road): The New York Public Library/ Art Resource, NY; 61: © 1978 Paul Hesse/mptvimages.com; 62–63 (FDR): iStockphoto.com/PictureLake, (Depression): New York Times Co./Hulton Archives/Getty Images, (card): iStockphoto.com/Kameleon007, (Leon): Courtesy of the Gorman Family personal collection, (poster): Courtesy of the Library of Congress, Prints & Photographs Division; 64–65 (grandkids): Photo by George Strock/Time & Life Pictures/Getty Images; 69 (George W. Bush): AP Photo/Pat Wellenbach, (Julia Roberts):

Bauer Griffin, LLC, (Bill Clinton): Courtesy of L.L.Bean, (Rachel McAdams): © Splash News www.splashnews.com; 77: Photo by George Strock/Time Life Pictures/Getty Images; 80–81: Courtesy of llbean.com; 82: © K.J. Historical/ Corbis; 83 (Gawtry): Lincoln Benedict, (Bergh): Courtesy of Peter Bergh; 84–85 (Doris Day): Silver Screen Collection/Getty Images, (record): © Robyn MacKenzie, 2011. Used under license from Shutterstock.com, (stamps) Courtesy of the Library of Congress, Prints & Photographs Division, (ENIAC): © Corbis, (Charlie Brown): iStockphoto.com/ilbusca, (VW): iStockphoto.com/ ilbusca; 89 (Kingfield): personal collection of Elmer Porter and Josephine Porter Cunningham; 90–91: Courtesy of the Saturday Evening Post; 102: (Bean, Me): Courtesy of Yankee Magazine, (Bonanza): Courtesy of Business Week, (salmon): Courtesy of Sports Illustrated, (Fortune): Courtesy of Fortune Magazine; 104–105: Courtesy of L.L.Bean; 108: © Bettmann/ Corbis; 109: D.Corson/Roberstock; 116–117 (Elvis): © Bettman/Corbis, (JFK): © Bettman/Corbis, (Vietnam): © Bettman/Corbis, (Lucy): CBS Photo Archive/Getty Images, (Berlin Wall): Popperfoto/ Getty Images; 131: Pat Wellenbach/AP Photo; 132–133 (Kent State): © Bettmann/Corbis, (Oil Embargo): © Bettman/Corbis, (Coty Award): Peter Dennen/Aurora Open, (Annie Hall): Photo by United Artists/Getty Images, (moon landing): NASA Kennedy Space Center (NASA-KSC), (calculator): © Gerald Bernard, 2011. Used under license from Shutterstock.com, (car): Photo by Barbara Freeman/Getty Images; 134 (Leon): Mimi Cotter; 141 (hunter): Courtesy of llbean.com; 147: Michael Haber; 151 (man): Foster Huntington, (driver): David Maher, (twitter fan): Courtesy of L.L.Bean; 153 (red hat): Courtesy of llbean. com; 154: Drawing by Donald Reilly, ©The New Yorker Magazine, Inc.; 155: © Bill Epperidge; 156 (storefront): Lincoln Benedict, (canoes, fish): Carl D. Walsh/Aurora Photos; 159: © WWD/Conde Nast/ Corbis; 160: Photos by Andree Kehn; 161 (bridesmaids, mink coat): Courtesy of llbean.com; 162: © Kevin Fleming/Corbis; 166–167 (Chris): © James Marshall/Corbis, (Cosbys): © NBC/Photofest,

(Katahdin): Courtesy of L.L.Bean, (computer): SSPL/Getty Images, (Olympics): Focus on Sport/ Getty Images; 174–175: Laura Doss; 177 (grandkids, red pack): Courtesy of llbean.com; 178–179 (bus ad): Courtesy of Gaslight Advertising Archives; 183: Nathan Bilow/ALLSPORT/Getty Images; 187 (home): © Roy Rainford/Robert Harding World Imagery/Corbis, (snowballs, sprinkler): © Ocean/Corbis, (statue): © Kevin Fleming/Corbis; 189: Photo by Rick Dean; 190–191 (Cobain): Frans Schellekens/Redferns/Getty Images, (kids): Courtesy of L.L.Bean, (Olympics): © Wally McNamee/Corbis, (Napster): Chris Hondros/Newsmakers/Getty Images, (DVD): iStockphoto.com/HSNPhotography; 192 (boat): Courtesy of Heidi McGee, (Reva): Courtesy of Reva Oliner; 194: Lincoln Benedict; 195 (Theresa): Alan Boutot; (bikes): Lincoln Benedict, (Joan): Alan Boutot; 196 (kayaks): Lincoln Benedict, (Tim): Lincoln Benedict, (Rogers): Alan Boutot; 197 (Jim): Courtesy of L.L.Bean, (lunch hour): Lincoln Benedict; 198 (Kurt): Lincoln Benedict, (Charlene): Alan Boutot; 199 (slideshow): Lincoln Benedict, (Becky): Alan Boutot, (Judy): Alan Boutot; 200 (Studio 1912): Courtesy of L.L.Bean, (Lee): Courtesy of Jim Gorman, (George): Alan Boutot; 201 (Charlotte): Alan Boutot; 202 (coffee): Lincoln Benedict, (shelves): Courtesy of L.L.Bean; 203 (boat and tote): Courtesy of Jim Gorman, (Stockholm): iStockphoto.com/scanrail, (Roe): Alan Boutot; 206: Lincoln Benedict; 207: Daymion Mardel; 208 (man): Daymion Mardel; 213: Courtesy of Tom Yarbrough; 216 (boat and tote): Courtesy of L.L.Bean, (Signature): Daymion Mardel, (Olympics): Timothy A. Clary/AFR/Getty Images; (Facebook): iStockphoto.com/gmutlu, (Obama): Chuck Kennedy/AFP/Getty Images; 217 (Costa Rica): Courtesy of Juan Carlos Catalan, (bridge): Courtesy of Tom Armstrong, (bus): Courtesy of the National Park Service; 218–219: Tom Rafalovich; 220: Lincoln Benedict; 223 (tent): Tom Rafalovich, (all kids): Laura Doss.

ACKNOWLEDGMENTS

L.L.Bean would like to thank:
Jason Bean, Richard Bulman, Tom Canney, Lisa Chesaux, Jake Christie, Alex Carlton, Zack Jones, Deb McCormack, Marcia Minter, Ruth Porter, Benedetta Spinelli, and Phil Uhl.

Melcher Media would like to thank:
Chika Azuma, Anne Calder, John Clifford, Holly Dolce, Shannon Fanuko, Melissa Goldstein, Jim Gorman, Megan Gorman, Amelia Hennighausen, Diane Hodges, Paul Kepple, Myles McDonnell, Carolyn Merriman, Rachel Post, Hollis Smith, Julia Sourikoff, Shoshana Thaler, and Megan Worman.